DR. ART ULENE'S
LOW-FAT
COOKBOOK

Art Ulene, MD

Recipes by Mary Ward

Health
POINTS™

PRESS

1995

Photographs Copyright © 1993 Amy Reichman, N.Y.C.

Seven recipes in this book are Copyright © 1993 Corning Consumer Products Company, and are reprinted with permission. These recipes include Chicken with Tarragon, Halibut with Confetti Sauce, Papaya Salad, Pasta with Fresh Tomatoes, Ratatouille, Red Beans and Rice and Strawberry Tart.

Nutritional values for the recipes in this book have been computed using Nutritionist III ™, Version 7.2, First DataBank (formerly N-Squared Computing), San Bruno, California.

Published by Health POINTS, 16601 Ventura Blvd., Encino, CA 91436

ISBN: 0-932513-03-4

Printed in USA by Banta/Viking Press

10 9 8 7 6 5 4 3 2 1

EDITOR: KUKLA VERA
ART DIRECTION: MARY LYNNE BARBIS
DESIGN/ ILLUSTRATION: PATRICK RASKE
    BARBIS & RASKE, LOS ANGELES
EDITORIAL / PRODUCTION STAFF: RICHARD TRUBO
    JAMIE MCDOWELL
    ROBIN RENICK

TABLE OF CONTENTS

INTROD

If you are one of those people who associates a low-fat dietary program with deprivation and dullness, get ready for a pleasant surprise. You are about to discover how easy and delicious low-fat cooking can be. If you'd like a hint of what to expect, glance through the following pages for a sample of the foods you'll be able to eat every day by using the recipes in this book. These recipes were designed to help you reduce the amount of fat you eat — helping you control your weight, decrease your cholesterol and cut your risk of heart disease.

U C T I O N

Even more important than the recipes in this book are the principles behind them. As you put these principles to work on a regular basis, you will see why we are able to say that you can decrease the amount of fat you eat without any great sacrifice. In the pages that follow, you will learn some basic concepts and techniques you can apply to all of your cooking. Use them to modify your favorite old recipes or to create brand new ones. We'll begin by reviewing the scientific reasons behind the movement to low-fat cooking.

Actually, in modest amounts, fats are an important element of a well-balanced diet. They perform many essential physiological functions: They are a source of energy, they act as building blocks for vital substances made by the body and they aid in transporting compounds such as fat-soluble vitamins (A, D, E and K) throughout the body. Every cell in your body needs fat, so you must have some fat in your diet to stay healthy.

But Americans eat too much fat, which is one reason why so many of us are overweight and why high blood cholesterol problems are so common. In fact, fat comprises about 37 percent of the average American's total calories; that's almost twice as much as we recommend to keep your weight and cholesterol level under control. Fats are a much more concentrated source of calories than carbohydrates or protein; each fat gram supplies 9 calories, while a gram of carbohydrate or protein provides only 4 calories. Thus, by shifting to low-fat eating, you can actually eat larger quantities of food without gaining weight or raising your cholesterol level.

There are several health benefits to low-fat eating. Studies have linked a high-fat diet not only to heart disease, but also to several types of cancer (of the colon, breast and possibly the ovary, uterus and prostate). And high-fat diets contribute to obesity, which increases your risk of developing high blood pressure and diabetes. So eating a low-fat diet can benefit you in many important ways.

There are three types of fat — saturated, monounsaturated and polyunsaturated. Saturated fats are the biggest contributor to heart disease, because they raise blood cholesterol levels. But when weight loss is your primary goal, you need to cut back on all three types of fat. They are all 100 percent fat, and they are equally poor choices for someone who is trying to lose weight. Their chemical structures may differ, but all of them contribute to putting extra fat on your body, so you can't overdo your consumption of any of them.

MAKING THE MOST OF THESE RECIPES

The recipes in this book have been carefully developed to help you lower the fat in your diet without giving up the pleasure of eating. To achieve this goal, I called upon Mary Ward to create the recipes. Mary was well qualified for this task. Mary, her husband and their three children have always been committed to a healthy lifestyle. The recipes in this book reflect Mary's lifelong commitment to low-fat, healthy eating.

The ingredients you'll find in these recipes are widely available in most supermarkets. They come from a variety of food groups, so they'll help you maintain a balanced diet while reducing your fat intake. And if you think that cooking healthy involves more work, think again: You will find these recipes just as easy to prepare as the higher-fat ones you have probably relied on for years.

To help you use these recipes and adapt other recipes in a reduced-fat way, Chapter 1 will present information in the following areas:

1. How to substitute more healthful ingredients for those that are high in fat.

2. How to extend your dishes with low-fat foods, and enhance them with flavorings and seasonings that are free of fat or low in fat.

3. How to alter your cooking techniques to produce healthier dishes.

Once you become familiar with these guidelines, you can apply them to any other cookbook on your kitchen shelf. You don't need to throw out those old recipes; just adapt them in the manner you'll read about here.

So turn the page and get started on the path to delicious and healthy dining. The low-fat dishes in this book are all appetizing and attractive. Try them, and you will see how easy and enjoyable low-fat eating can be.

Best wishes for good eating and good health.

Art Ulene, MD

ADAPTING RECIPES

C H A P T E R • O N E

As we promised in the Introduction, you don't have to sacrifice good eating to reduce the fat in your diet. Lower-fat meals can be delicious and easy to prepare. In this chapter, you'll find specific recommendations for transforming a recipe high in fat into one that is low in fat. With some smart substitutions, you can continue to use your favorite cookbooks, making them allies in your efforts toward low-fat eating. Some of the alterations are obvious, such as substituting non-fat milk for whole milk, roast chicken for fried chicken and jam for butter on your toast. Others may not be quite as evident, but they are just as simple to make. And perhaps surprisingly, in most cases, you will retain the flavor of the original dishes in these recipe make-overs.

FOR FAT REDUCTION

NOW LET'S GET DOWN TO SPECIFICS:

MEATS

You do not need to completely eliminate red meat from your diet to gain control over your weight. But because meat can be high in fat, you should choose lean cuts. For beef, that means substituting sirloin, round, chuck, loin, flank or extra-lean ground beef; in particular, look for cuts that have the least amount of visible white fat (marbling) in the muscle; streaks of fat indicate a higher-fat cut of meat.

The best pork choices are tenderloin, leg (fresh), shoulder (arm or picnic) and boiled ham. When buying lamb, choose cuts of leg, arm, rib or loin. All trimmed cuts of veal are acceptable, except those that are commercially ground. Also check the grade of meat. The label USDA "select"indicates that the meat is lower in fat than "choice" or "prime"; "select" varieties are also tasty and rich in protein and iron, and thus should be your first choices.

POULTRY

Ounce for ounce, chicken is lower in fat than nearly all cuts of beef, particularly if you remove the skin. So consider poultry as a frequent substitute for meat in your recipes. Ground or shredded chicken and turkey can be utilized in a number of imaginative ways. For instance, use them (instead of ground beef) to make meatballs, meatloaf, chili, tacos, spaghetti sauce or any of your other favorite ground-beef recipes.

Keep in mind, however, that unless you have turkey ground to order, it probably won't be as low in fat as you think. Manufacturers of commercially ground turkey are allowed to grind some of the turkey skin in with the ground turkey, which increases the fat content by as much as 15 percent. Removing the skin of chicken or turkey before serving is very important, and a way to reduce the amount of fat by more than half. Even if you're already in the habit of taking off the skin, you can lower your fat intake even more by choosing light over dark meat. For example, while 43 percent of the calories of skinless dark chicken meat come from fat, only 23 percent of the calories in skinless light chicken meat are fat calories. Breast meat tends to be the leanest portion of the chicken.

SEAFOOD

Most fish have less fat than red meat and poultry. In general, the fat content of fish with dark flesh is higher than that of fish with lighter flesh. Those particularly low in fat include halibut, cod, sea bass, snapper, haddock, flounder and perch. Many types of shellfish (clams, scallops, crab, lobster) are also quite low in fat. If you buy canned tuna, be sure it is packed in water instead of oil; this can cut the fat content by as much as 80 percent.

CHEESE

As a rule, cheese must be selected carefully and eaten sparingly. Most cheeses are brimming with fat, which makes up a staggering 65 to 75 percent or more of their calories. A single ounce of hard cheese like Swiss contains nearly 8 grams of fat! Even cheese that's labeled "low-fat" or "part-skim" might surprise you. Part-skim ricotta, for example, gets 51 percent of its calories from fat, while reduced-fat mozzarella cheese has a 39 percent fat content. There are about 3 grams of fat in one ounce of reduced-fat mozzarella, which is about the same amount of fat as in a three-ounce portion of skinless, light-meat chicken. Nevertheless, there are ways to reduce your fat intake and still eat cheese.

When you're making substitutions in recipes that call for some of the harder, higher-fat cheeses, for example, using those with strong flavors will allow you to cut down on the amount you use. Also, if you grate cheese, you will probably eat less of it. Grated parmesan, cheddar and sapsago cheeses can be sprinkled on main dishes and casseroles, allowing you to add taste without consuming too much fat. Feta cheese is another good choice, sprinkled in a salad or on top of a casserole. Other acceptable, lower-fat substitutions are part-skim mozzarella and Romano; they'll work just as well in your recipes as their higher-fat counterparts. But remember that hard cheeses should be eaten in limited amounts, even the part-skim varieties.

By the way, there are also many "fat-free" cheeses now available—containing 0 grams of fat! However, some people are unhappy with the unusual consistency, flavor and texture of non-fat cheeses, preferring instead to use the reduced-fat varieties, but in smaller quantities.

Check the labels of the cheeses you're thinking of using and keep this guideline in mind: Any cheese with more than 2 grams of total fat per ounce must be eaten sparingly.

OTHER DAIRY PRODUCTS

Milk is an excellent source of protein, vitamins and minerals in every gulp. But you've got to be careful about which kind of milk you buy. At first glance, the differences between the varieties of milk—whole milk (3.3 percent fat by weight), low-fat (2 percent or 1 percent), and non-fat or skim (nearly free of fat)—don't seem that dramatic. But calculations by weight can be deceiving. The differences may not seem like much—until you look at grams of fat and calories.

Each cup of whole milk contains just over 8 grams of fat. That adds up to 74 calories per cup, which means that 49 percent of the calories in whole milk come from fat. In spite of its name, low-fat milk still contains almost 5 grams of fat, so 35 percent of its calories come from fat. By contrast, nonfat or skim milk contains less than one-half gram of fat per cup. Clearly, then, when recipes call for milk, you're much better off choosing non-fat. Non-fat milk works very well in soups, sauces, puddings and baked products. By the way, in recipes that call for half-and-half or heavy cream, evaporated skim milk is an excellent alternative. It has the same rich, creamy texture, but only a trace of fat. You can even whip it, but make certain that the milk (as well as the bowl and the beaters) are well chilled before you begin.

Other substitutions in this category are just as easy to make. For example, when a recipe calls for sour cream, try low-fat or non-fat yogurt or yogurt cheese instead; your taste buds probably won't know the difference. A cup of non-fat yogurt has 0 grams of fat, while an equal amount of regular sour cream contains a staggering 42 grams! A combination of cottage cheese and buttermilk works, too. Use yogurt as a topping for chili or baked potatoes, or in place of mayonnaise in a salad dressing. It also makes a flavorful base for a dip. Or try it in place of sour cream in soups and sauces. Be aware, though, that yogurt tends to separate if overheated. To keep that from happening, add the yogurt at the end of the cooking time and warm gently. Or prior to heating, mix one tablespoon of cornstarch into a cup of yogurt.

OILS

If you're concerned about your coronary arteries, you probably already know that you're better off avoiding saturated fats and cooking instead with monounsaturated oils like olive oil and canola oil, or polyunsaturated oils like corn oil and safflower oil. But don't forget: All fats inflict similar damage when your goal is weight control. All oils are 100 percent fat! A single tablespoon of any oil contains about 13.5 grams of fat and about 120 calories—every one of them a fat calorie. So, the less oil you consume, the better.

When recipes call for oil, you can usually reduce the amount you use significantly without hurting the taste and consistency. The key is to cut back slowly—one tablespoon of oil at a time each time you make the recipe, until you notice a real difference. By the way, don't be tempted to pour on a product that advertises itself as "100% vegetable oil," as if that means it's healthy. Although vegetables themselves are generally very low in fat, the same can't be said for vegetable oil, which is 100 percent fat.

USING FOOD EXTENDERS

Food extenders are low-fat ingredients that can be mixed into your favorite dishes; in the process, they will dilute or stretch a main ingredient that is high in fat. That means you can still enjoy the primary ingredient, but each serving will have less fat in it (assuming you keep the portion size constant).

Some of the best food extenders might already be right in your refrigerator. Grains (and products made from grains), vegetables, fruits, beans and lentils all make great extenders—and they've been used successfully this way for centuries. If meat dishes are among your favorites, the addition of these extenders to recipes will allow you to reduce the amount of meat (and fat) per portion, while still preserving the basic identity of the dish. For instance, by adding grains (rice, barley) or vegetables (potatoes, carrots, tomatoes) to a meat recipe, you won't give up the robust nature of the dish, but your fat intake will decline. In the same way, using beans to replace some of the meat in a chili recipe will dilute the amount of fat per serving.

Meat recipes are not the only dishes that can be extended this way. If you're preparing a "creamy" soup, use cooked, pureed vegetables instead of the cream. With a meat-based soup or stew, the addition of beans and lentils will make you forget that you've decreased the amount of meat.

USING FOOD ENHANCERS

Because fat is an important contributor to the flavor of foods, you'll need to compensate for the diminished taste of low-fat dishes by adding other sources of flavor. Food enhancers are low-fat ingredients that are very flavorful. Fresh dried herbs and spices are a good place to start for flavor enhancement. Experiment with a wide variety of them, and find out which ones please your palate most.

Dill and parsley are favorites of many people, particularly on foods such as fish, poultry and vegetables. Enhancers like garlic, ginger, onions and shallots can also make low-fat foods more appealing; for example, just a teaspoon of fresh, chopped herbs can be added to several servings of vegetables, giving their flavor a real boost. To provide extra "bite" for some of your recipes, try adding a little red or green sweet pepper. For an even stronger flavor, rely on hot peppers, salsa, mustard or hot sauce.

Other popular options are wine vinegar, or a mellow vinegar like balsamic. For skinless chicken dishes, spicy marinade can add pungency. And to garnish salads or rice dishes, bean sprouts—or sprouts from wheat seeds or alfalfa seeds—are excellent choices. When adding flavor to traditional foods like baked potatoes, leave the butter and sour cream in the refrigerator, and choose lower-fat enhancers instead. We already suggested non-fat yogurt as a substitute for sour cream; but to boost the taste of the yogurt, add some fresh dill, parsley, scallions, green pepper or chives. If you want an alternative to yogurt, a few tablespoons of stewed tomatoes or spicy tomato salsa will give baked potatoes a unique flavor, or top the potato with a combination of dried herbs and a small amount of lemon juice. On the topic of lemons, keep a few fresh ones in your refrigerator; a little squeeze can give flavor to all kinds of foods.

While flavor enhancers need not be fresh, many people find that the extra effort fresh ingredients may require are worthwhile. For example, use a peppermill for freshly ground black pepper. Other fresh spices—from garlic to ginger root—can be purchased in many grocery stores, and they'll remain fresh for weeks.

COOKING TECHNIQUES FOR LOW-FAT EATING

Your best efforts at choosing low-fat foods can be undermined in the kitchen if you prepare your meals in ways that increase the fat content. You can start with the healthiest ingredients, but if they're cooked improperly, all of your efforts will be sabotaged. To lay claim to a new, fat-reducing style of cooking, here are some important guidelines:

COOKING MEATS, POULTRY AND FISH

Frying

Avoid frying whenever possible. It increases a food's fat content significantly. When you're frying chicken, for instance, some of the oil is absorbed by the chicken. At the same time, the fat within the meat cannot drain away during cooking. By contrast, the alternatives listed below allow the fat to drip off, so it will be lost rather than ending up in your body where it can subvert your weight-loss efforts.

Broiling

Foods that you might have pan-fried in the past should be broiled instead. Meatballs are a good example; when broiled, their fat will drip into the pan below, so you're not frying them in their own fat. Potato slices can also be broiled, creating low-fat French fries; or broil eggplant slices to create eggplant parmigiana.

Roasting

Meats should be roasted in a preheated oven set at about 350° F.
That's a temperature low enough to encourage the fat to drip off.
(At higher temperatures, the meat will be seared, and it will retain
the fat.) To keep lean meat moist while cooking, baste it with a
fat-free liquid such as fruit juice marinade or soy sauce.

Baking

Although similar to roasting, baking uses a covered container in the
oven. This is a particularly good approach for less fatty cuts of meat,
but you may need to add some cooking liquid.

Poaching

This is a good choice for cooking fish. You don't need a special fish
poacher to use this technique; a regular skillet will work just as well.
Make sure you add enough liquid (broth, wine, water seasoned with
lemon or dill) to cover the fish itself. Cook until the fish is fork-tender.

Steaming

Try steaming fish in a steamer basket placed in a pan large enough to
accommodate it. Put some water—seasoned with herbs, wine or other
flavorings—into the pan, and then insert the steamer with the fish in it.
The cooking time should be about one minute for each ounce the
fish weighs.

Sauteing

When a recipe recommends sauteing, you'll usually cut the food into
small pieces and cook it uncovered over high heat. Instead of cooking
oils or fats, try liquids such as wine, flavored vinegars, unsweetened
fruit juice or defatted chicken (or vegetable) broth. Or coat the pan with
a vegetable-oil spray. (These sprays are now marketed with flavors of
their own, such as olive oil or butter flavoring.)

COOKING VEGETABLES, LEGUMES AND LENTILS

Vegetables contain very little fat, and your goal should be to keep them that way. Avoid the temptation to cook them in butter or oils, or to smother them with high-fat sauces. Also, select cooking techniques that preserve as much of the natural nutrition of these foods as possible. These include:

Steaming

Although boiling is a common way to cook vegetables, many vitamins and minerals are lost in the process. This depletion of nutrients is much less likely to occur with steaming. Put vegetables in a steamer basket once the water (about 1 inch deep) is boiling; after the vegetables are in place, reduce the heat so the water is simmering. Place the lid on the pot, making sure that the water does not touch the food during cooking. When the vegetables start to become tender—but still retain some crispness—they are ready to eat. The usual cooking time is 5 minutes for most vegetables cut in serving sizes.

Stir-frying

When you stir-fry vegetables, which involves cooking them in very intense heat, they retain their color, texture and nutrients. There's another advantage as well: Only a little bit of oil is needed to stir-fry. Even better, try using small amounts of broth, wine or lemon juice. Pour the liquid around the edges of the wok (or heavy skillet), and once it is hot, place the vegetables (sliced, diced or minced) into it. Stir the food constantly, making sure it is slightly coated to seal in the juices. You may need to add more liquid before cooking is complete.

Microwaving

Like steaming, microwave cooking keeps vitamin loss to a minimum. Follow the instructions that come with your oven for specific cooking times.

Cooking Oils

As you've already read, oils—whether saturated, polyunsaturated or monounsaturated—are all the same when it comes to caloric content and weight control. So, although you'd lean toward an unsaturated fat when trying to protect your coronary arteries, all cooking oils are on a level playing field when you're attempting to shed excess pounds. Look for alternatives to oils whenever you can. You can cut the amount of fat in your dishes by using non-stick vegetable oil cooking spray or non-stick cookware. If you use conventional oil, don't pour it into your pan; instead, apply it with a brush to avoid using too much. All you need is a very thin coat, just enough to keep the food from sticking.

OTHER WAYS TO LIMIT FAT

Here are some additional suggestions for low-fat food preparation. Trim away all visible fat before cooking meat. Because you can't cut out the fat within the meat, be especially conscientious about buying the leanest cuts possible. With poultry, remove not only the skin, but all of the visible fat as well. If you're convinced that chicken without skin is not worth eating, give the following a try: Dip the skinless chicken parts in skim milk, and roll them in crushed oat bran cereal to coat the surface. Then bake them and enjoy the tasty results. Soups, stews and sauces should be refrigerated before using, so the fat in them will rise to the top and congeal. You can then easily skim off the fat before reheating. For each tablespoon of fat you remove from the surface, you'll eliminate 120 fat calories.

THE NEW FOOD LABELS

Since 1994, new "Nutritional Facts" labels have been placed on most food wrappers and packages. When you're trying to determine the fat content of particular items, these uniform and streamlined labels can make this process relatively simple. While there's lots of information on the labels, only a few numbers are important when trying to keep track of the fat in your diet.

Look for two values on the labels: *Calories* (the total calories in the stated serving size) and *Calories from Fat* (the number of fat calories in the serving size). Take these two figures, and divide the number of calories from fat by the total calories. Then, multiply this result by 100 to change it to a percentage — namely, the percentage of calories that comes from fat. Thus, if a particular food has 250 calories, and 50 calories from fat, divide 50 by 250. Multiply the answer (.20) by 100 — 100 x .20 = 20%. In this example, 20 percent of the calories come from fat. The lower the percentage of fat, the better.

If you are trying to lose weight, significantly cut back on the number of foods you consume with fat calories of 30 percent or more, and increase your intake of those with 10 percent fat calories or less. When foods fall into the middle ground—11 to 29 percent of calories from fat—eat them carefully and thoughtfully

ADAPTING YOUR RECIPES TO LOWER THE AMOUNT OF FAT

Almost any recipe can be changed to lower its fat level. As a general rule, start cooking with half the fat called for in a recipe. Add more only if you need it (you probably won't!). In most cases, the chemistry of the recipe will not be altered by this fat reduction. Vegetables with strong aromas (such as onions and peppers) can boost the flavor of dishes in which the fat has been minimized.

Let's look at specific examples of how recipes can be adapted in low-fat ways, using many of the approaches we've already described in this chapter. In each case, the recipes on the right side of the page also appear in more detail later in the book, complete with preparation methods. In this section, however, we'll look at how easy it is to take a high-fat recipe and cut its fat significantly.

Turn to Non-Stick Cookware

The use of non-stick cookware is one of the most important moves you can make to lower the fat in your diet. This cookware doesn't have to be expensive, but the label does need to say "non-stick coating."

For example, substituting a non-stick pan in place of a regular frying pan allows you to saute with much less oil. In fact, only 2 teaspoons will keep most vegetables from sticking and burning when using a non-stick pan. In most recipes, this will save you over 15 grams of fat.

CHOOSE LOWER-FAT INGREDIENTS

New low- and non-fat food items are being added to supermarket shelves every week—from cheeses to yogurt to pasta. Most of these products are quite good and easy to cook with, although the non-fat cheeses tend to clump rather than melt when cooked. As you shift to low-fat cooking, do some taste testing of your own along the way; trial and error will help you find items and brands that work best for you. When selecting meat, always look for extra-lean ground beef, chicken or turkey. In the following PASTA WITH MEAT SAUCE recipes, the use of extra lean ground beef — the only change in the ingredient list— reduces total fat by 75 percent.

PASTA WITH MEAT SAUCE

Serves: 10

(see preparation method in Pasta Chapter)

REGULAR GROUND BEEF

2 teaspoons olive oil

4 cloves garlic, minced

1 large onion, chopped

1 pound regular ground meat

6 ounces tomato sauce

28 ounces crushed tomatoes

1/2 cup dry red wine

2 tablespoons fresh herbs

Calories: 496
Calories from fat: 30%
Total fat: 16 grams

EXTRA-LEAN GROUND BEEF

2 teaspoons olive oil

4 cloves garlic, minced

1 large onion, chopped

1 pound extrta-lean ground beef

6 ounces tomato sauce

28 ounces crushed tomatoes

1/2 cup dry red wine

2 tablespoons fresh herbs

Calories: 355
Calories from fat: 11%
Total fat: 4 grams

SAVVY SUBSTITUTING

In most recipes, simple low-fat substitutions can make a dramatic difference in your overall fat intake. When the recipe calls for a whole egg, try 2 egg whites. When it calls for cream, choose yogurt, buttermilk or light evaporated milk instead. When butter, margarine or cooking oil is in the recipe, decrease the amount to 1 to 2 teaspoons. And if ground beef is called for, as in the following recipe, substitute ground turkey breast. When you dine on these MEXICAN STYLE MEATBALLS, you'll never guess that the meat you are eating is ground turkey breast and that the binding agent is egg whites. And look at all the fat you'll save!

MEXICAN STYLE MEATBALLS

Serves: 4

(see preparation method in Appetizers Chapter)

GROUND BEEF & WHOLE EGG

1 egg
1 pound ground beef
1/4 cup cilantro, chopped
1 onion, chopped
2 cloves garlic, minced
2 jalapeno peppers
1/2 teaspoon cumin
2 large tomatoes
4 ounces green chilies

Calories: 331
Calories from fat: 67%
Total fat: 25 grams

GROUND TURKEY BREAST & EGG WHITES

2 egg whites
1 pound ground turkey breast
1/4 cup cilantro, chopped
1 onion, chopped
2 cloves garlic, minced
2 jalapeno peppers
1/2 teaspoon cumin
2 large tomatoes
4 ounces green chilies

Calories: 146
Calories from fat: 15%
Total fat: 1 grams

If you occasionally want to consume a higher-fat meat, cut the portion size, and add a low-fat extender such as potatoes, beans, rice or pasta. This strategy is used often in this book so that certain higher-fat entrees may be used. In the following TRADITIONAL CHATEAUBRIAND recipe, on the left side of the page, you will find cream and butter in the potatoes and larger portions of steak. The LIGHT CHATEAUBRIAND, on the right, uses more potatoes, low-fat ingredients on those potatoes and smaller amounts of tenderloin.

CHATEAUBRIAND

Serves: 2
(see preparation method in Meat Chapter)

TRADITIONAL

2 small potatoes, baked
2 tablespoons butter
1/4 cup cream
2 tenderloin steaks,
  8 ounces each
baby vegetables

Calories: 727
Calories from fat: 51%
Total fat: 42 grams

LIGHT

2 large potatoes, baked
1/2 cup low-fat yogurt

2 tenderloin steaks,
  4 ounces each
baby vegetables
herb sprigs

Calories: 495
Calories from fat: 16%
Total fat: 9 grams

COATINGS

Many people think that coatings—such as those used in the VEAL SCALLOPINI, TURKEY CROQUETTES, PORK STIR FRY and EGGPLANT PARMIGIANA recipes in this book—are strictly taboo for low-fat cooking. Not true. For coating, try using flour, followed by an egg white binder and then bread crumbs. The egg white binder will crispen as it cooks, and the bread crumbs will end up with a crunch of their own. Use only a tiny bit of fat and a non-stick frying pan.

Here are high- and low-fat EGGPLANT PARMIGIANA recipes that use flour, egg (or egg whites) and bread crumbs. Notice the impressive difference in total fat content between them.

EGGPLANT PARMIGIANA

Serves: 6

(see preparation method in Vegetarian and Side Dishes Chapter)

HIGH-FAT EGGPLANT PARMIGIANA

1 large eggplant (2 pounds)
1 cup all-purpose flour
1 cup bread crumbs
1/2 cup grated parmesan cheese
2 cloves garlic, minced
4 whole eggs
1 cup oil

1 cup mozzarella cheese, shredded
Fry in oil; then bake

Calories: 855
Calories from fat: 51%
Total fat: 49 grams.

LOW-FAT EGGPLANT PARMIGIANA

1 large eggplant (2 pounds)
1 cup all-purpose flour
1 cup bread crumbs
1/4 cup grated parmesan cheese
2 cloves garlic, minced
1 egg
4 egg whites
2 tablespoons oil
1/2 cup mozzarella cheese, shredded
Saute in a little oil; then bake

Calories: 442
Calories from fat:18%
Total fat: 9 grams.

OTHER HINTS FOR REDUCING FAT IN YOUR DIET

Don't be locked into traditional thinking about certain foods and dishes. For example, you can approach meat as a flavoring instead of a staple. In most recipes, you can cut the amount of meat in half, while increasing vegetables or carbohydrates at the same time.

Here are a few other meat-related tips:

❑ When a recipe includes bacon, either eliminate it entirely or decrease it considerably. If the recipe calls for 1 pound of bacon, use no more than 1/4 pound. When you cook the bacon, either microwave it until crisp or fry it until very crisp. Drain it to make sure all external fat has been removed. In a bacon, lettuce and tomato sandwich, use just 1 slice of bacon, and crumble it on top of the tomato to make it stretch.

❑ The longer you cook meat, the more fat it will lose. So meat that is cooked medium or well-done will typically end up with less fat than meat served rare. By the way, lean cuts tend to cook more rapidly than fattier beef, requiring about 20 percent less cooking time.

❑ Non-oil marinades tend to have a pleasant, light and herbal appearance. For meat, a tenderizer (wine or fruit juice) plus stock and herbs make a great marinade. A good rule of thumb is to use 50 percent wine or fruit juice and 50 percent stock. Shift your outlook on other foods and food-preparation methods as well, in order to eliminate as much fat as possible, but still keep the dishes tasty. For example:

❑ Be creative in your use of oil and butter in order to keep your fat consumption to a minimum. You may believe, for instance, that a bechamel (or white) sauce needs equal proportions of fat and flour—about 2 tablespoons of each for every cup of water—but this isn't true. A delicious sauce can be made from 1/4 cup of flour, cornstarch or arrowroot blended with water, milk or stock. In the case of certain bland sauces, such as the gravy for the TURKEY CROQUETTES (see recipe in Poultry Chapter), a little pat of butter or a splash of a delicious olive oil rounds out the sauce and provides good mouth feel.

❑ With even a tiny amount of fat and a non-stick pan, foods can be browned. When foods that naturally contain some sugar (tomatoes, onions) are browned intensely, a dark, carmel-like substance will form, creating delicious, interesting flavors. If you are using tomato paste or sauce in a recipe, try this: Rub the tomato paste around the bottom of a non-stick pan. Heat the pan until it's very hot. When the paste starts to brown and blacken, remove the pan from the heat source. Add a flavorful stock, vegetable water or wine to collect the flavorful bits, and continue with the recipe.

❏ The use of vegetable waters is a low-fat cooking technique adopted with great success by many chefs. It simply requires draining the vegetables and saving their water. This water may be added to stock, used in place of stock in your favorite recipes or reduced and used as gravy.

❏ To create vegetable water (as in the CAPELLINI A LA CHECCA recipe in Pasta Chapter), chop juicy vegetables such as cucumber, zucchini, tomatillos and onion with a couple of ripe tomatoes. Add a teaspoon of salt and allow to sit and cure for several hours. The flavorful water may be used as a base for dressing pasta or as a sauce base.

❏ When certain foods are covered while cooking for long periods of time, they break down in ways that create a soft, flavorful stew. This stewing brings out hidden flavors with no additional fat. For instance, in recipes using beans, try cooking the beans to the point where they begin to break down, thus providing their own flavorful "gravy." Summer squashes can be blended with oregano and basil and then stewed; they'll produce a delicious paste that can be used on pasta, as a topping for pizza or as a sandwich filling.

❏ Eliminate butter on the dinner table. When choosing a spread for bread or rolls, use jam or jelly instead. Toppings for French toast and pancakes need not include butter, either; use applesauce or fresh fruit. See the FRUIT SAUCE recipe (Breakfast Chapter) for a healthy alternative to syrup.

❏ When eating a salad, place the low-fat salad dressing on the side and use it sparingly. Or better still, use non-fat dressing or a squeeze of lemon in place of the dressing. When you make your own salad dressing, cut the oil in the recipe by at least half.

❏ When snacking, choose low-fat options such as fresh fruit or cut-up raw vegetables. Also, see the recipes in the Appetizers Chapter for SALSA WITH CHIPS and dips made with SOUR CREAM SUBSTITUTE and YOGURT CHEESE.

YOU ARE...

STRAWBERRY TART

(For recipe see Desserts Chapter)

ABOUT TO

HALIBUT WITH
CONFETTI SAUCE
(For recipe see Fish & Shellfish Chapter)

DISCOVER...

GAZPACHO

(For recipe see Soups & Stews Chapter)

HOW EASY

RATATOUILLE

(For recipe see Vegetarian & Side Dishes Chapter)

AND TASTY...

BAKED
TARRAGON CHICKEN
(For recipe see Poultry Chapter)

LOW-FAT

RED BEANS AND RICE
(For recipe see Vegetarian & Side Dishes Chapter)

COOKING ...

PASTA WITH
FRESH TOMATOES
(For recipe see Pasta Chapter)

CAN BE!

PAPAYA SALAD
(For recipe see Salad Chapter)

A P P E T

C H A P T E R · T W O

Today, people expect and enjoy ultra-light foods such as these appetizers. The variety of low-fat, tasty products in the supermarket has increased tremendously over the last few years. Use these recipes to lighten up your appetizer tray.

IZERS

For starters, here are two good alternatives for sour cream in any recipe.

SOUR CREAM SUBSTITUTE

Serves: 4

1/4 cup buttermilk
3/4 cup 1% milk-fat cottage cheese
1 teaspoon lemon juice

Blend in the blender until smooth.
Use this for dips, in cooking and in salads. It has good dairy texture and flavor.

Nutritional Information per Serving
Calories 35; Calories from Fat 14%; Total Fat less than 1 g; Saturated Fat less than 1 g;
Cholesterol 2 mg; Sodium 188 mg

YOGURT "CHEESE"

Serves: 3

2 cups non-fat yogurt

Fill yogurt strainer or colander lined with a kitchen towel or cheesecloth with yogurt.
Tie together ends of towel or cheesecloth, strain yogurt, hanging it over a bowl.
Strain overnight or up to one day, allowing yogurt to lose excess moisture.

The thick yogurt remaining in the towel or cloth is the yogurt "cheese."
It has a rich consistency and works especially well in dips.

Nutritional Information per Serving
Calories 60; Calories from Fat 14%; Total Fat less than 0 g; Saturated Fat less than 0 g;
Cholesterol 0 mg; Sodium 85 mg

BAKED NEW POTATO APPETIZER WITH YOGURT, ONION AND PARSLEY

Serve as directed, or cool and split the potatoes, make a hole in each and pipe dressing into the hole with a pastry tube. Garnish with a tiny bit of red caviar.

Serves: 24 appetizer servings

24 tiny, blemish-free new red-skinned potatoes, scrubbed
1 1/2 cups yogurt cheese
1 small red onion, finely minced
3 tablespoons finely chopped parsley
1 tablespoon sweet wine (Riesling), optional
salt and pepper to taste

Preheat oven to 350° F. Arrange potatoes in 1 layer on a baking sheet. Bake until tender, 20 to 30 minutes. Serve immediately (or store in an insulated container, hot, for up to 6 hours).

TO SERVE: Blend yogurt cheese with onion, parsley and sweet wine. Season. Place yogurt dressing in a large bowl with potatoes surrounding it.

QUICK AND EASY: Use low-fat sour cream substitute to replace yogurt cheese.

Nutritional Information per Serving
Calories 35; Calories from Fat 7%; Total Fat less than 1 g; Saturated Fat less than 1 g;
Cholesterol 1 mg; Sodium 13 mg

BAYOU SHRIMP REMOULADE

Here's an appetizer that you can prepare up to 2 days in advance. It is filling and nutritious.

Serves: 6

1/3 cup tarragon vinegar
1 tablespoon catsup
2 tablespoons freshly grated horseradish
**   (or prepared horseradish sauce)**
1 teaspoon prepared mustard
2 teaspoons Cajun seasoning
4 scallions, sliced with tops

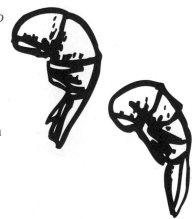

2 large tomatoes, chopped
1 1/4 cups celery, chopped
1 pound medium-sized cooked, cleaned shrimp
6 cups shredded salad greens (iceberg lettuce, romaine lettuce,
  gourmet lettuces)

In a medium-sized bowl, combine and whisk the vinegar, catsup, horseradish, mustard, Cajun seasoning and onions. Add tomatoes, celery and shrimp and stir to coat. Marinate in refrigerator for 4 to 5 hours.

TO SERVE: Arrange 1 cup lettuce on each of the 6 salad plates. Arrange the shrimp and sauce over lettuce.

Nutritional Information per Serving
Calories 109; Calories from Fat 7%; Total Fat 1 g; Saturated Fat less than 1 g;
Cholesterol 147 mg; Sodium 215 mg

DILLED GRAVLAX ON WHOLE WHEAT MELBA

These are a great choice for holiday entertaining as they have such a festive appearance. Buy the best quality smoked salmon available.

Serves: 24 appetizer servings

1 whole-wheat baguette, sliced into very thin slices (48 rounds)
1 tablespoon olive oil (or a mixture of olive oil and hot oil)
1 tablespoon sesame seeds
8 ounces smoked salmon
8 ounces non-fat evaporated milk
1 teaspoon lemon juice or orange juice
2 to 3 tablespoons horseradish
1 8-ounce package reduced-fat cream cheese, softened
1/4 cup fresh dill (or 2 tablespoons dry)
fresh dill and pimiento for garnish

To make melba: Preheat oven to 250° F. Place baguette slices on a cookie sheet. Brush a tiny bit of oil onto each one. Sprinkle with sesame seeds. Bake for 1 hour. Store in a tightly-sealed plastic bag.

In a food processor fitted with steel blade, chop salmon finely (or finely chop by hand). Add milk in a steady stream until all is absorbed. Add lemon juice, horseradish, cream cheese and dill and blend until combined. Chill for at least 1 hour.

TO SERVE: Divide mixture among whole-wheat rounds. Garnish with a little dill and pimiento.

QUICK AND EASY: Use commercially prepared onion melba rounds.

Nutritional Information per Serving
Calories 84; Calories from Fat 20%; Total Fat 2 g; Saturated Fat less than 1 g; Cholesterol 3 mg; Sodium 203 mg

HONEY CHICKEN BITES

Instead of cutting the chicken into small, bite-sized pieces, slice them into 4 x 1 inch strips —then skewer them onto 6 inch bamboo sticks. These delicious bites always bring rave reviews.

Serves: 12, as an appetizer

2 whole chicken breasts, boned and skinned
**   (about 1 pound)**
6 tablespoons honey
2 tablespoons teriyaki marinade
1 teaspoon seasoned salt
1 clove garlic, minced
juice of 1 lime

Cut each boned breast into bite-sized pieces. Blend honey with marinade, seasonings, garlic and lime juice. Pour over chicken pieces and marinate (a few hours or overnight). Bake at 350° F for 30 minutes, turning once to brown evenly.

TO SERVE: Place on tiny crackers garnished with herbs, on a leaf of French endive or on a tray with snow peas.

Nutritional Information per Serving
Calories 58; Calories from Fat 8%; Total Fat less than 1 g; Saturated Fat less than 1 g; Cholesterol 11 mg; Sodium 99 mg

HUMMUS

This Mid-Eastern dip is so quick and easy to make. Serve it with pieces of pita bread, with vegetable crudite or as a spread on crackers. The secret to a great tasting hummus: richly toasted sesame seeds.

Serves: 8

1/4 cup sesame seeds
1 can (15 ounces) garbanzo beans with liquid
1 clove garlic, sliced into 3 pieces
1 freshly squeezed lemon (3 tablespoons lemon juice)
1 teaspoon salt
1 small onion, chopped
sesame seeds for garnish
chopped green onions for garnish
8 pita rounds, separated and toasted

In a small skillet, toast sesame seeds over high heat. Stir and shake pan as it heats to evenly toast sesame seeds.

Place sesame seeds in a blender cup. Add remaining ingredients, cover and blend on low for 30 seconds. Uncover and stir. Blend on high for 1 minute or until the mixture is smooth.

TO SERVE: Pour into a decorative 2-cup bowl. Garnish with remaining sesame seeds and chopped green onions. Serve with a variety of vegetable crudite, melba rounds or toasted pita bread.

Nutritional Information per Serving
Calories 151; Calories from Fat 19%; Total Fat 3 g; Saturated Fat less than 1 g;
Cholesterol 0 mg; Sodium 640 mg

MARINATED PORK STICKS

This recipe originated in the Philippines and may be used as a main course when served with rice.

Serves: 12 appetizer servings or 6 main course servings

1 tablespoon low-fat peanut butter
1 cup chicken stock
1/4 cup lite soy sauce
4 cloves garlic
1/2 teaspoon freshly grated pepper
2 pounds pork tenderloin, trimmed of any fat
24 4-inch bamboo sticks
12 tiny pita rounds

Place peanut butter, soy sauce, garlic and pepper in a blender cup.
Blend until smooth.

Slice meat into 24 strips about 1/2 inch wide by 4 to 5 inches long. Skewer meat strips in zigzag fashion on bamboo sticks. Place sticks in a plastic bag and pour marinade over all. Marinate overnight (or for at least 3 hours).

Heat charcoal or other grill to medium hot. Grill sticks for 5 minutes a side basting with marinade.

TO SERVE: Let guests make their own tiny pita sandwiches, by sliding 2 sticks into each piece of pita.

QUICK AND EASY: Use well-trimmed, precut stir-fry pork.

Nutritional Information per Serving
Calories 157; Calories from Fat 19%; Total Fat 3 g;
Saturated Fat 1 g; Cholesterol 53 mg; Sodium 389 mg

MEXICAN STYLE MEATBALLS

Ground turkey breast meat is lean, low in fat and very tasty. This appetizer recipe teams ground turkey with Mexican spices for a wonderfully nutritious treat. Prepare this in the microwave!

Serves: 4

1 pound ground turkey breast meat
2 egg whites
1/4 cup cilantro, chopped
1 medium-sized onion, chopped
2 cloves garlic, minced
2 fresh or canned jalapeno peppers,
   medium or hot, chopped
1/2 teaspoon cumin
2 large tomatoes
1 can, 4-ounces green chilis, diced
1/2 cup cilantro, chopped
1 teaspoon salt

Combine the ground turkey with the egg whites, cilantro, onion, garlic, jalapeno peppers and cumin. Mix with hands until the mixture holds together well. Form into 2 to 3 dozen meatballs.

Place the meatballs on a microwave-safe tray, and microwave on high for 10 to 12 minutes or until the meatballs are cooked and firm. Turn the tray frequently. Remove the meatballs to a serving platter, discarding the fat. (If using the conventional method, bake the meatballs on a jellyroll pan at 350° F for 30 minutes.)

Meanwhile, in a blender cup or food processor, blend the tomatoes, canned chilis, cilantro and salt until very smooth.

Place salsa in a 2-cup microwave bowl and microwave on high for 3 minutes, just until hot. Spoon the hot salsa over meatballs and serve immediately. (If using conventional method, pour the salsa over the meatballs, stir and heat for 5 more minutes.)

Nutritional Information per Serving
Calories 146; Calories from Fat 15%; Total Fat 1 g; Saturated Fat less than 1 g;
Cholesterol 70 mg; Sodium 425 mg

PISSALADIERE

The name Pissaladiere refers to food served on a crust. Unlike a pizza, the flavors come from the blend of vegetables and herbs. This one serves a crowd!

Serves: 24 appetizer servings

2 packages (5/16-ounce each) active dry yeast
1 1/2 cups very warm water
3 1/2 cups white flour (or a combination of
    white, wheat and bread flour)
2 teaspoons salt
1 egg, beaten
3 pounds onions, peeled and chopped
2 tablespoons olive oil
8 ripe tomatoes (or 28-ounce can plum tomatoes, drained)
2 cloves garlic, chopped
1/3 cup black olives, chopped
salt and pepper to taste
herb leaves to garnish

In a medium bowl, dissolve yeast in water. Blend flour, salt and egg, then add yeast mixture to it. Knead until smooth and satiny, adding more water if necessary. Shape dough into a ball, place in a floured bowl or pan, cover with a towel and let rise for 1 hour.

To make filling, cook the onions in oil over low heat until soft and golden, about 45 minutes. Do not brown. Add tomatoes and garlic and cook until water is evaporated. Season with salt and pepper.

Preheat oven to 400° F. Grease a large, 11 x 17 inch cookie sheet. Roll yeast crust to fit cookie sheet. Spoon on filling and sprinkle with olives. Allow to rise for 15 minutes. Bake at 400° F for 20 minutes, then reduce to 350° F for 20 minutes or until crust is done.

Serve warm or at room temperature on a platter garnished with fresh herbs.

QUICK AND EASY: Use 2 loaves frozen prepared bread dough in place of above crust.

Nutritional Information per Serving
Calories 112; Calories from Fat 16%; Total Fat 2 g; Saturated Fat less than 1 g;
Cholesterol 0 mg; Sodium 122 mg

PIZZA ON THE GRILL WITH ROASTED PEPPERS AND THREE CHEESES

Pizza is quick, easy and nutritious. In this recipe, the roasted peppers give it color as well as flavor. Try other toppings such as zucchini and chopped olives, sliced tomatoes and garlic, or a very light coating of basil pesto.

Serves: 12 (2 pizzas cut into 6 slices each)

1 package (5/16 ounce) active dry yeast
3/4 cup very warm water
2 cups flour (a blend of wheat, white, cornmeal
   and bread flour)
1 teaspoon salt
1/2 teaspoon sugar
oil and cornmeal for pizza pans
2 cups roasted red, green and
   yellow pepper strips
2 ounces low-fat mozzarella cheese,
   shredded
1/4 cup parmesan cheese, grated
1/4 cup Romano cheese, grated

Blend yeast with water and allow to rest for 5 minutes. Add flour, salt and sugar, and mix until dough is shiny and firm, about 5 minutes. (This may be done in a food processor or mixer fitted with a dough hook.) Cover dough with a damp cloth and allow to rise in a warm place for 10 minutes.

Meanwhile, heat oven to 500° F (for Pizza on the Grill, heat charcoal grill very hot). Divide dough and roll into 2 10-inch rounds. Place on 2 10-inch pizza pans which have been oiled and sprinkled with cornmeal.

Top with peppers and cheeses. Place in hot oven (or onto grill) and bake for 5 minutes or until dough is just set. Slide pizza directly onto oven rack (or grill rack) and continue baking for 5 to 7 minutes until crust is nicely browned and cheeses are melted.

QUICK AND EASY: Use frozen bread or pizza dough.

Nutritional Information per Serving
Calories 129; Calories from Fat 20%; Total Fat 3 g; Saturated Fat 2 g;
Cholesterol 6 mg; Sodium 297 mg

SPRING ROLLS

Usually, spring rolls are deep-fried, making them heavy and laden with fat. Baking spring rolls is a much better alternative — it allows the taste and crunch of the filling to really come through.

Serves: 8

8 ounces cooked chicken breast, shredded,
2 tablespoons soy sauce
1 egg white
1 tablespoon cornstarch
2 tablespoons chicken stock
2 cups finely chopped vegetables (include garlic, scallions,
  mushrooms, bean sprouts, pea pods, celery, bok choy)
8 egg roll wraps
non-stick cooking spray
teriyaki and mustard dipping sauces

Blend chicken with soy sauce, egg white and cornstarch. Heat chicken stock in a non-stick frying pan. Add chicken mixture and saute chicken. Add vegetables. Cook until vegetables are tender but crisp.

Portion 1/8 of the mixture diagonally into each egg roll. Fold up corners, then roll. Preheat oven to 375° F. Coat a baking tray with non-stick cooking spray. Place egg rolls in pan and bake for 15 minutes, until brown.

TO SERVE: Place on individual plates with small ramekins of teriyaki and mustard dipping sauces.

Nutritional Information per Serving
Calories 100; Calories from Fat 9%; Total Fat 1 g;
Saturated Fat less than 1 g; Cholesterol 22 mg;
Sodium 310 mg

STEAMED CLAMS OR MUSSELS

This recipe is so simple yet so tasty and nutritious. Use plenty of bread to sop up all that delicious, garlicky sauce.

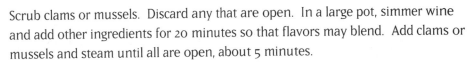

Serves: 4

2 pounds clams or mussels (or a combination)
1 cup dry white wine
1 cup onion, chopped
2 cloves garlic, chopped
1 cup celery, chopped
4 tablespoons chopped fresh oregano (or parsley)
few sprigs oregano for garnish
8 slices crusty Italian bread

Scrub clams or mussels. Discard any that are open. In a large pot, simmer wine and add other ingredients for 20 minutes so that flavors may blend. Add clams or mussels and steam until all are open, about 5 minutes.

TO SERVE: Divide clams among four deep bowls, including broth with each. Garnish with oregano and Italian bread rounds.

Nutritional Information per Serving
Calories 168; Calories from Fat 5%; Total Fat 1 g; Saturated Fat less than 1 g;
Cholesterol 29 mg; Sodium 227 mg

TOMATO (OR CUCUMBER) SALSA WITH CHIPS

Homemade salsa is very nutritious — with vitamin A, vitamin C and fiber. If you toast your own chips, you'll have an appetizer that is nutritious and tasty.

Serves: 10

10 corn tortillas
2 very ripe large tomatoes (or 2 large cucumbers, peeled)
1/2 cup fresh cilantro
2 tablespoons jalapeno peppers
1/4 teaspoon salt

Preheat the oven to 400° F. Cut each tortilla into 8 pieces. Place on an ungreased cookie sheet. Bake for 15 minutes or until the chips are browned and crisp. Cool.

Meanwhile, cut the tomatoes into 8 wedges. Place the tomatoes in a blender cup along with the cilantro, the jalapenos and the salt. Pulse several times until salsa is very smooth, about 1 minute. Serve immediately or store in refrigerator until serving.

QUICK AND EASY: Use commercially prepared, baked tortilla chips.

Nutritional Information per Serving
Calories 74; Calories from Fat 15%; Total Fat 1 g; Saturated Fat less than 1 g;
Cholesterol 0 mg; Sodium 135 mg

VEGETABLE CAVIAR

Black olives are full of fat. But used in small amounts, they add almost a meat feel to a dish. They are used well in this recipe.

Serves: 8

2 ounces ripe olives, chopped and drained
8 ounces green chilis (mild or hot), chopped
1/4 cup cilantro, chopped
2 large, ripe tomatoes, seeded and chopped
1/4 cup cucumber, peeled and chopped
1/4 cup scallions, sliced
2 teaspoons balsamic vinegar
salt to taste
cilantro sprigs for garnish
8 ounces baked tortilla chips

Combine all ingredients.

TO SERVE: Drain off excess liquid, garnish with cilantro sprigs and serve with tortilla chips.

Nutritional Information per Serving
Calories 92; Calories from Fat 20%; Total Fat 2 g;
Saturated Fat less than 1 g; Cholesterol 0 mg; Sodium 533 mg

BREA

C H A P T E R • T H R E E

Breakfast eating styles vary widely across the country. In this chapter are some favorite (but lightened-up) restaurant-style dishes such as Corned Beef Hash, Broccoli Quiche and Vegetable Omelet. Also, we've included some breakfast drinks — a good way to start the day when you want to "keep it light."

Breakfast is a very important meal. Try these recipes and enjoy.

KFAST

APPLE BERRY FIZZ

Here's a winning combination: It is a complete breakfast in a glass, rich with dietary fiber.

Serves: 1

1 cup canned apple juice
1/2 cup strawberries or raspberries, fresh or frozen
1/2 cup ice cubes (if using frozen berries,
  use water instead of ice cubes)
1/2 cup club soda

Place the apple juice, berries and ice cubes or water into a blender cup. Blend until smooth, about 30 seconds.   Pour into a 16-ounce glass; stir in club soda; serve immediately.

Nutritional Information per Serving
Calories 161; Calories from Fat 5%; Total Fat less than 1 g; Saturated Fat less than 1 g; Cholesterol 0 mg; Sodium 58 mg

APPLE WAFFLES WITH FRUIT SAUCE

These waffles are best when made in a Belgian waffle iron, although any waffle iron will do. Wrap and freeze any waffles you don't eat!

Serves: 12

1 package (5/16 ounce) active dry yeast
1/2 cup very warm water (115° F)
non-stick cooking spray
3 1/2 cups white or wheat flour
1 teaspoon baking powder
1/3 cup light brown sugar, packed
3/4 teaspoon salt
1 cup apple juice, room temperature

4 large egg whites
1 tablespoon oil
1 to 2 cups water

Blend the yeast with very warm water. Allow mixture to cure for 5 minutes until the yeast is bubbly.

Spray the grids of the waffle iron with non-stick cooking spray and preheat for 10 minutes.

Blend the flour with baking powder, brown sugar and salt. Mix the apple juice with the egg whites and oil. Mix the yeast with the apple juice mixture and gently fold the flour into this mixture. Allow to rise in a warm place for 15 minutes.

Just before baking waffles, add 1 to 2 cups water to make the waffles thick, but pourable. Place 1/2 cup of the waffle batter into each side of the Belgian waffle maker. Spread the mixture with a spatula so that it covers the waffle grid. Close the lid and allow the waffle to bake until no more steam arises from the waffle maker. This will take 5 to 8 minutes. When you open the waffle maker, the waffles should release easily. Serve the waffles hot with Fruit Sauce (next page), or serve cold with fruit, frozen non-fat yogurt or low-fat cottage cheese.

Belgian waffles can be frozen for up to 3 months or refrigerated for 3 weeks. To reheat: microwave each waffle 30 seconds (high) or place waffle in 350° F oven for 5 to 7 minutes.

Nutritional Information per Serving
Calories 254; Calories from Fat 10%; Total Fat 3 g; Saturated Fat less than 1 g;
Cholesterol 0 mg; Sodium 275 mg

FRUIT SAUCE FOR PANCAKES OR WAFFLES

Here's a healthy alternative to heavy and artificially flavored maple syrups.
Keep a supply in the freezer and reheat it when serving pancakes or waffles.

Serves: 12

2 cups fresh or frozen strawberries, thawed
1 cup sliced kiwi fruit, peeled
2 ripe bananas
1 cup fresh or frozen blueberries, thawed
1/2 cup pure maple syrup
1 cup water

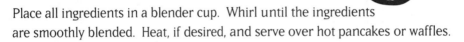

Place all ingredients in a blender cup. Whirl until the ingredients
are smoothly blended. Heat, if desired, and serve over hot pancakes or waffles.

Nutritional Information per Serving
Calories 78; Calories from Fat 4%; Total Fat less than 1 g; Saturated Fat less than 1 g;
Cholesterol 0 mg; Sodium 10 mg

BROCCOLI CRABMEAT QUICHE

Replace traditional pastry crust with frozen Filo dough, and you have a tender crust
without much fat.

Serves: 8

2 sheets Filo dough, defrosted and wrapped in damp towel
non-stick cooking spray
1 bunch broccoli, separated into flowerets, peeled and sliced
4 scallions, chopped
6 ounces crabmeat (fresh, frozen or canned), drained
1/4 cup fresh parsley, chopped
1/4 cup provolone cheese, shredded
8 large egg whites
1 1/3 cups low-fat buttermilk
1 teaspoon Dijon mustard
1/4 teaspoon paprika

Remove a sheet of Filo dough from damp towel. Double and place over 9-inch pie plate. Spray a little non-stick cooking spray between layers. Repeat with second sheet of Filo. Trim to fit. Bake unfilled crust at 375° F for 10 minutes to crisp crust. (The crust will puff slightly.)

Steam or microwave broccoli for 4 minutes, until it is bright green in color and is still crunchy. Drain. Blend broccoli with scallions and parsley. Distribute evenly over the Filo pastry. Sprinkle cheese over the broccoli mixture. Whip eggs with buttermilk, mustard and paprika. Pour over quiche. Bake for 10 minutes at 375° F; reduce heat to 350° F and continue baking for 20 minutes longer. Let stand for 5 minutes before cutting. Cut into 8 wedges to serve.

FOR VEGETABLE QUICHE: Add 1 cup broccoli, 1 cup steamed sweet peppers and 1 cup steamed, sliced mushrooms.

Nutritional Information per Serving
Calories 92; Calories from Fat 17%; Total Fat 2 g; Saturated Fat 1 g;
Cholesterol 27 mg; Sodium 345 mg

CORNED BEEF HASH

Here is a recipe for those who love a special weekend breakfast that includes corned beef hash — but without all the fat. Leftovers are excellent when reheated at 400° F for 20 minutes.

Serves: 4

2 cups beef stock
1/2 cup onion, chopped
1/2 green pepper, seeded and diced
1 rib celery, chopped
1 clove garlic, minced
4 ounces very lean, sliced corned beef, finely shredded
2 medium-sized baking potatoes, baked and diced

In a large non-stick skillet, heat stock. Add onion, pepper, celery and garlic and poach until vegetables are tender. Add corned beef and potatoes and poach until all liquid is absorbed. Meanwhile, preheat broiler. Broil corned beef hash about 4 inches from broiler heat for a few minutes to crisp. Cut into 4 wedges and serve immediately.

Nutritional Information per Serving
Calories 143; Calories from Fat 19%; Total Fat 3 g; Saturated Fat 1 g;
Cholesterol 18 mg; Sodium 332 mg

FRESH TOASTED GRANOLA

This recipe is an absolute favorite; it's rich with dietary fiber and so delicious that you'll want to make extra to give to your friends!

Serves: 24 1/2-cup servings

1 cup oat bran hot cereal
2 cups rolled oats
2 tablespoons almonds, sliced
2 tablespoons sunflower seeds
2 tablespoons sesame seeds
1/4 cup non-fat dry milk
2 tablespoons dark brown sugar, packed
1/2 teaspoon cinnamon
1/2 cup maple syrup
1/2 cup seedless raisins

Preheat oven to 300° F.

In a large bowl, combine oat bran, rolled oats, almonds, sunflower seeds, sesame seeds, dry milk, brown sugar and cinnamon. Pour maple syrup mixture over dry ingredients and blend thoroughly.

Spread granola in a rimmed, ungreased 10 x 15-inch jellyroll pan and bake for 45 minutes, stirring every 10 minutes. It is important to stir the granola every 10 minutes to blend flavors and toast granola evenly. Stir in raisins and bake an extra 10 minutes. Remove from oven and cool. Store in an airtight container for up to 3 months. Serve granola with non-fat milk or sprinkled atop non-fat frozen yogurt.

Nutritional Information per Serving
Calories 108; Calories from Fat 18%; Total Fat 2 g; Saturated Fat less than 1 g;
Cholesterol 1 mg; Sodium 13 mg

FROZEN PINEAPPLE REFRESHER

A refreshing way to start any day — not only is it low fat but also low calorie and high fiber.

Serves: 2

1 cup fresh pineapple pieces (or canned
  or frozen)
1/2 cup orange juice
1 banana
1 cup ice cubes
1 cup club soda

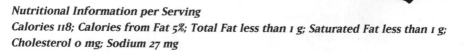

Place pineapple, orange juice, banana and ice cubes in a
blender cup. Blend until smooth, about 30 seconds.
Pour into two 16-ounce glasses. Stir in club soda.

Nutritional Information per Serving
Calories 118; Calories from Fat 5%; Total Fat less than 1 g; Saturated Fat less than 1 g;
Cholesterol 0 mg; Sodium 27 mg

FRUIT COMPOTE

*A true fruit compote needs five different fruits. You may use fresh, canned, frozen
or a variety. Leftovers may be blended in the blender for a breakfast drink.*

Serves: 4

1 cup fresh strawberries, sliced
1 banana, sliced
1 cup melon, cubed
1/2 cup blueberries or raspberries
1/2 cup canned mandarin oranges, drained

Nutritional Information per Serving
Calories 72; Calories from Fat less than 1%; Total Fat less than 1 g;
Saturated Fat less than 1 g; Cholesterol 0 mg; Sodium 5 mg

ITALIAN FRITTATA

Make this frittata in advance. Just before serving, quickly saute vegetables,
add eggs, cook and finish with cheese. This is good!

Serves: 6

non-stick cooking spray
1 cup zucchini, scrubbed and chopped with peel
1/3 cup green pepper, seeded and chopped into 1/4-inch chunks
1/3 cup onion, chopped coarsely
1 large tomato, chopped into 1/2-inch pieces
1 teaspoon dried oregano
1 tablespoon fresh basil, chopped (or 1 teaspoon dried basil)
1/4 teaspoon black pepper
1/2 cup whole-wheat elbow macaroni, cooked
12 egg whites, beaten to blend
2 tablespoons Romano cheese, freshly shredded

Spray a large skillet with non-stick cooking spray. Heat to hot. Reduce heat, cover
and saute the zucchini, pepper and onion until tender, about 8 minutes, stirring
occasionally. Add chopped tomato. Stir in the oregano, basil, pepper
and macaroni.

Preheat broiler. Pour the eggs over the zucchini-tomato mixture. Cook until the
egg bottom is set, about 5 minutes. Place the frittata under the broiler about 4
inches from heat. Broil for 2 minutes. Sprinkle with the cheese and broil until the
cheese melts.

Cut into wedges and serve hot.

Nutritional Information per Serving
Calories 56; Calories from Fat 19%; Total Fat 1 g;
Saturated Fat less than 1 g; Cholesterol 4 mg; Sodium 102 mg

ITALIAN OMELET

To prevent the omelet from sticking to the pan, finish the omelet under the broiler.
It puffs up and has a beautiful, colorful appearance.

Serves: 2

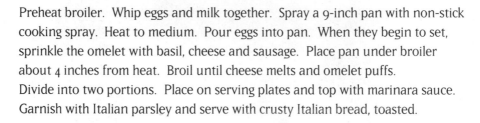

4 egg whites
1 whole egg
1 tablespoon non-fat milk
non-stick cooking spray
**1/4 cup fresh basil, chopped (or 2 teaspoons
    dry basil)**
1/4 cup low-fat mozzarella cheese, shredded
**4 ounces turkey-breast sausage, cooked
    and chopped***
3/4 cup non-fat marinara sauce, heated
Italian parsley
2 thick slices crusty Italian bread, toasted

Preheat broiler. Whip eggs and milk together. Spray a 9-inch pan with non-stick
cooking spray. Heat to medium. Pour eggs into pan. When they begin to set,
sprinkle the omelet with basil, cheese and sausage. Place pan under broiler
about 4 inches from heat. Broil until cheese melts and omelet puffs.
Divide into two portions. Place on serving plates and top with marinara sauce.
Garnish with Italian parsley and serve with crusty Italian bread, toasted.

*If turkey-breast sausage is not available in your area, brown 4 ounces ground
turkey breast meat with 1/2 teaspoonful dry oregano, 1/4 teaspoon black pepper
and 1/4 teaspoon ground thyme.

Nutritional Information per Serving
Calories 333; Calories from Fat 19%; Total Fat 7 g; Saturated Fat 4 g;
Cholesterol 154 mg; Sodium 514 mg

STRAWBERRY SMOOTHIE

Here's another breakfast in a glass — it's rich in fiber and vitamins, and moderate in calories.

Serves: 2

1/2 cup orange juice, fresh or frozen
1 very ripe banana
1 cup fresh or frozen (unsweetened) strawberries
1/2 cup non-fat milk
1 cup ice cubes (if using frozen strawberries,
   use water instead of ice cubes)

Place the orange juice, banana, strawberries, milk and ice cubes in a blender cup. Blend until smooth, about 30 seconds. Pour into two 12-ounce glasses. Serve immediately.

Nutritional Information per Serving
Calories 176; Calories from Fat less than 5%; Total Fat 1 g; Saturated Fat less than 1 g;
Cholesterol 1 mg; Sodium 34 mg

SUNSHINE-STYLE FRENCH TOAST

Using orange juice to replace egg yolks is a great idea—it adds a sparky flavor, a golden color and helps to brown the bread.

Serves: 4, 2-piece servings

1/2 cup non-fat milk
6 egg whites
2 tablespoons sugar
1/2 cup orange juice
1 teaspoon orange peel, grated
8 1/2-inch-thick slices day-old French bread or wheat bread
non-stick cooking spray
1/4 cup powdered sugar
1/2 cup maple syrup

In medium-sized mixing bowl, beat milk, egg whites, sugar, orange juice and orange peel until the mixture is thick, blended and smooth. Pour the mixture into a shallow bowl.

Dip the bread slices into the egg mixture and allow to rest on a large jellyroll pan. Make sure all of the egg mixture is utilized on the 8 bread slices.

Spray a large griddle or a large skillet with non-stick cooking spray. Heat to medium hot (about 325° F). Without crowding, brown the toast slices on both sides. Allow at least 5 minutes per slice to insure cooking throughout. Dust with the powdered sugar. Serve with hot maple syrup or Fruit Sauce (see recipe for Fruit Sauce earlier in this chapter).

Nutritional Information per Serving
Calories 299; Calories from Fat 5%; Total Fat 1.5 g; Saturated Fat less than 1 g; Cholesterol less than 1 mg; Sodium 315 mg

VEGETABLE OMELET

This picture-perfect omelet is heavy on the vegetables and light on the cheese.

Serves: 2

8 egg whites
1 tablespoon non-fat milk
non-stick cooking spray
2 cups mixed vegetables, such as steamed broccoli, mushrooms,
    tomatoes and onions
1/4 cup low-fat American cheese, shredded
chopped parsley for garnish
2 slices 7-grain bread, toasted

Preheat broiler. Whip eggs and milk together. Spray a 9-inch pan with non-stick cooking spray. Heat to medium. Pour eggs into pan. When they begin to set, sprinkle the omelet with vegetables and cheese. Place pan under broiler about 4 inches from heat. Broil until cheese melts and omelet puffs.
Divide into two portions. Place on serving tray. Garnish with chopped parsley.

Nutritional Information per Serving
Calories 249; Calories from Fat 19%; Total Fat 5 g; Saturated Fat less than 1 g; Cholesterol 14 mg; Sodium 321 mg

WHOLE-WHEAT CREPES WITH FILLINGS

Here's a basic recipe for low-fat crepes, followed by two recipes for variations on crepe fillings. Make plenty of crepes, freeze or refrigerate, and you'll have a lot of great breakfast eating. You may fill these same crepes with fruit and yogurt for a great dessert!

Serves: 6, 2-crepe servings

1 cup whole-wheat or white flour
2/3 cup non-fat milk
6 large egg whites
1/4 teaspoon salt
non-stick cooking spray

Place all the ingredients with 3/4 cup water in a medium-sized bowl and mix thoroughly by hand or with an electric mixer. Refrigerate for 1 hour or overnight.

Spray a 5 or 6-inch non-stick crepe pan with a thick coating of non-stick cooking spray. Heat the pan over a medium hot burner. (If you are using an electric crepe pan, heat it to 375° F.) Pour 2 to 3 tablespoons crepe batter into the pan, tilting and swirling the hot pan as you add the batter. Use just enough batter to cover the bottom of the pan with a thick layer of crepe batter.

When the surface of the crepe is dry and the underside brown, turn the crepe. Allow other side to brown. This whole process will take about 5 minutes. Remove crepe and start a stack of crepes. Repeat with the remaining batter. As you stack the crepes, cover with plastic wrap.

Fill crepes and roll, or fill and fold edges in to form a square.

Nutritional Information per Serving
Calories 94; Calories from Fat 4%; Total Fat less than 1 g;
Saturated Fat less than 1 g; Cholesterol less than 1 mg;
Sodium 159 mg

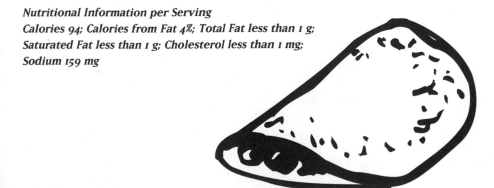

MEXI-CHICKEN CREPES

Here's south-of-the-border taste rolled in a crepe. This easy-to-make recipe is very low in calories and has a wonderful flavor. It is even better reheated the second day!

Serves: 6, 1-crepe servings

3 large, ripe tomatoes, chopped
1 tablespoon green chilis or jalapeno pepper
1/2 cup fresh cilantro, chopped
non-stick cooking spray
6 low-fat crepes *(see recipe on previous page)*
1 1/2 cups cooked chicken breast, cut into
    bite-size pieces
1/4 cup low-fat Monterey jack cheese, shredded
1/2 cup low-fat sour cream *(see recipe for low-fat sour cream in the
    Appetizers Chapter)*
3 green onions, chopped
sprigs of cilantro
salt to taste
freshly ground pepper

Place the chopped tomatoes with chilis or jalapenos and cilantro in a blender cup. Pulse several times with an on-off motion until slasa is chunky.

Spray a 9 x 9 inch baking dish with non-stick cooking spray. Spread half of the salsa mixture on the bottom of the baking dish.

Preheat the oven to 375° F. Place 1/4 cup of the chicken down the middle of each crepe and roll. Place seam side down in the baking dish atop salsa. Spoon remaining salsa over crepes. Sprinkle with cheese. Cover and bake for 25 minutes. Filling will be hot and cheese melted.

Spoon the sour cream down the centers of the crepes. Sprinkle with green onions. Garnish with sprigs of cilantro. Serve immediately. Salt and pepper to taste.

QUICK AND EASY: Use 3 cups of a good prepared salsa to replace first 3 ingredients.

Nutritional Information per Serving
Calories 217; Calories from Fat 12%; Total Fat less than 3 g; Saturated Fat 1 g;
Cholesterol 51 mg; Sodium 224 mg

ASPARAGUS AND MUSHROOM CREPES

*What could be more delightful: Fresh vegetables, light cheeses
and a sauce napped with wine. This recipe is a breakfast or brunch winner!
It is high in calcium, fiber and flavor.*

Serves: 6, 1-crepe servings

**1/4 cup chicken stock
2 cups fresh or frozen asparagus, sliced in 1-inch pieces
1 cup fresh mushrooms, sliced
1/2 teaspoon lemon juice
1 teaspoon fresh tarragon
non-stick cooking spray
6 low-fat crepes (*see recipe on page 55)*
2 tablespoons low-fat Swiss cheese
3 tablespoons cornstarch
1 teaspoon Dijon mustard
1 1/2 cups plain non-fat yogurt
1/4 cup dry white wine
2 tablespoons grated parmesan cheese
chopped chives and paprika for garnish**

Place chicken stock in a non-stick frying pan. Add the asparagus and
mushrooms and poach vegetables lightly for 5 minutes. Mix in the lemon juice and
fresh tarragon.

Preheat oven to 350° F. Spray a 9 x 9 inch baking dish with non-stick cooking spray.
Place 1/4 cup asparagus mixture down the center of each crepe, fold and lay side-
by-side, seam side down in the baking dish. Sprinkle with Swiss cheese.

Blend together the cornstarch with Dijon mustard, yogurt, white wine and the
parmesan cheese. Spoon this mixture on top of the crepes. Cover and bake for 30
minutes or until the sauce is lightly browned.

Garnish with chopped chives, paprika and freshly ground black pepper.
Serve immediately. Salt to taste.

*Nutritional Information per Serving
Calories 149; Calories from Fat 16%; Total Fat 3 g; Saturated Fat 1 g;
Cholesterol 8 mg; Sodium 224 mg*

S O U P S &

C H A P T E R * F O U R

Soups allow you to experiment with ingredients more than with any other dish. Try adding herbs, hot sauce, cayenne pepper and crunchy toppings such as baked tortillas, crushed crackers and homemade croutons. And, remember, soups are a delicious dish in winter and fall as well as spring and summer.

STEWS

A FEW WORDS ABOUT MAKING STOCK...

It's always preferable to make vegetable and meat stocks from scratch — they taste fresher, they are richer and they are not as loaded with salt as prepared stocks. Try the following recipe to make vegetable and meat stocks. When you're in a pinch for time, don't hesitate to use a prepared stock. When purchasing a prepared stock, look at the ingredient statement and select the stock with the least fat; some stocks, even bouillon cubes, are loaded with fat.

HOMEMADE STOCK

Makes 3 quarts (12 servings)

3 cups onion, chopped
2 cloves garlic, smashed
2 cups carrot chunks
2 cups celery tops with leaves
2 cups mushrooms
2 cups chunked zucchini
3 bay leaves
bouquet garni (cheesecloth filled with 6 peppercorns, fresh springs of thyme, basil leaves, parsley and other herbs; after filling cheesecloth, tie it and smash it with a meat cleaver to release volatile oils of herbs and to smash peppercorns)
3 pounds meat, poultry or fish bones (optional)
3 quarts water

In a large soup kettle or pressure cooker, blend all ingredients. Pressure cook for 30 minutes or simmer for 3 hours. Strain stock and season to taste.

Nutritional Information per Serving
Calories 14; Calories from Fat 8%; Total Fat less than 1 g;
Saturated Fat less than 1 g; Cholesterol 0 mg;
Sodium 6 mg

BEEF STEW WITH BARLEY

This stew is a hearty meal in a bowl, with lean chunks of beef, vegetables and tender barley. Serve this to your hungry friends with Minted Citrus Salad (see recipe in Salad Chapter) or with a tossed vegetable salad! It's delicious.

Serves: 6

non-stick cooking spray
1 pound beef stew meat, trimmed of all fat
4 cups beef stock (homemade or prepared)
1 cup pearl onions (fresh or canned)
1 teaspoon dry basil leaves
1/4 cup fresh parsley, chopped
1 1/2 cups barley, uncooked
1 1/2 cups carrots, sliced
salt to taste
freshly ground pepper

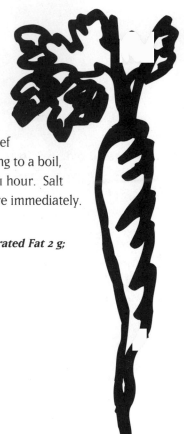

Spray a Dutch oven with non-fat cooking spray. Heat to hot. Add beef and brown on all sides. Remove beef to paper towels and pat off excess fat. Rinse Dutch oven.

In the Dutch oven, blend together browned beef, beef stock, onions, basil, parsley, barley and carrots. Bring to a boil, cover and reduce heat to simmer stew. Simmer for 1 hour. Salt and pepper to taste. Ladle into wide bowls and serve immediately.

Nutritional Information per Serving
Calories 346; Calories from Fat 16%; Total Fat 6 g; Saturated Fat 2 g;
Cholesterol 54 mg; Sodium 60 mg

BLACK BEAN STEW

This is an award-winning recipe for a hearty stew with little fat.

Serves: 10

1 12-ounce package black beans, washed
   and picked over
non-stick cooking spray
1 1/2 cups green onion, chopped with tops
3 cloves garlic, minced
1 26-ounce can tomatoes
1 cup fresh or canned pumpkin puree
   (not pumpkin pie filling!)
1 1/2 cups beef stock (homemade or prepared)
1 tablespoon cumin
1 1/2 tablespoons balsamic (or red wine) vinegar
8 ounces Canadian bacon, cut into small squares
1 cup dry sherry
1 cup yogurt cheese *(see recipe in Appetizers Chapter)*
sliced green onion for garnish
10 lime slices

Place the beans in a large saucepan and cover with boiling water to a level of
3 inches above the beans. Simmer until the beans are tender, about 3 hours. Drain.

Spray the large saucepan thoroughly with non-stick cooking spray. Saute the onion
and the garlic just until soft. Add the tomatoes, pumpkin puree, beef stock, cumin,
vinegar and black beans. Simmer for 25 minutes. Add the ham, black pepper, and
sherry and heat thoroughly. Salt to taste. Serve in large bowls with a dollop of low-
fat yogurt, a sprinkle of green onions and a slice of lime.

QUICK AND EASY: Use 1 19-ounce can Black Beans (Frijoles Negros), drained, in
place of the dry beans.

Nutritional Information per Serving
Calories 154; Calories from Fat 16%; Total Fat 3 g; Saturated Fat less than 1 g;
Cholesterol 15 mg; Sodium 490 mg

CLAM CHOWDER

This is the ultimate in Clam Chowders — it is hearty, rich, very flavorful and has only 11% calories from fat!

Serves: 6

6 dozen fresh clams, scrubbed (or 12-ounce can of chopped clams)
1 cup onion, chopped
3 tablespoons fresh thyme
3 bay leaves
1 cup dry white wine
3 cups chicken stock
3 cups potatoes, peeled and diced
1 cup leeks, sliced
1 package (10 ounces) frozen corn kernels
3 tablespoons cornstarch
1 cup yogurt cheese *(see recipe in Appetizers Chapter)*
4 ounces Canadian bacon, chopped into small pieces
sprigs of thyme for garnish

If you are using fresh clams, soak in cold water with a little cornmeal for 1 hour. Scrub shells of all sand.

In a large stock pot, poach onion, thyme and bay leaves in white wine. Add chicken stock and heat to boil. Steam clams in boiling stock just until they open, about 5 minutes. Remove clams; cool and remove their meat. If stock is at all sandy, strain through a very fine strainer or through several layers of cheesecloth.

Into stock, add potatoes and leeks and cook until tender, about 20 minutes. Add corn and continue to cook for 10 minutes. Blend cornstarch with yogurt cheese and 1/2-cup water and add it to the stock pot, gradually, whisking for a smooth sauce. Reheat with Canadian bacon and clams.

TO SERVE: Pour hot chowder into serving bowls and garnish with sprigs of thyme.

Nutritional Information per Serving
Calories 272; Calories from Fat 11%; Total Fat 3 g; Saturated Fat 1 g;
Cholesterol 42 mg; Sodium 383 mg

GOLDEN LENTIL SOUP WITH POTATOES

This soup is so easy to prepare, and it's packed with flavor and good nutrition.

Serves: 12

12 ounces golden lentils, picked over and cleaned
8 cups beef stock (homemade or prepared)
1 can (16 ounces) tomatoes, chopped
  with liquid
2 tablespoons parsley, chopped
1 large onion, diced
1 bay leaf
2 cloves garlic, crushed
2 medium carrots, sliced thin
4 medium red potatoes, cubed with skins
chopped tomato for garnish
parsley sprigs for garnish

In a large soup pot, combine the lentils with the beef stock, tomatoes, parsley, onion, bay leaf and garlic. Bring to a boil, reduce heat, cover and simmer for 1 hour until lentils are tender. Add carrots and potato and more water as necessary to maintain the same level of liquid. Cook for an additional 30 minutes, stirring occasionally until potatoes are tender. Salt and pepper to taste. Remove bay leaf before serving.

TO SERVE: Ladle into serving bowls. Top each bowl with chopped tomato and a large sprig of parsley.

Nutritional Information per Serving
Calories 120; Calories from Fat 3%; Total Fat less than 1 g; Saturated Fat less than 1 g;
Cholesterol 0 mg; Sodium 74 mg

ITALIAN SOUP

This recipe has lots of ingredients but is well worth the time and effort it takes to prepare.

Serves: 8

5 cups beef stock (homemade or prepared)
1 cup dry red wine
1 pound low-fat, Italian turkey-breast sausage
1 cup onion, chopped
2 cloves garlic, minced
1 cup carrots, sliced
1 cup celery, chopped
1 green pepper, chopped
2 cups chopped tomatoes
   (or 16 ounces canned)
8 ounces tomato sauce
1 teaspoon fresh oregano
several sprigs thyme
8 ounces frozen or fresh tortellini
freshly chopped basil and parsley for garnish
1/4 cup grated parmesan cheese for garnish

In a stock pot, heat stock and wine. Add sausage and simmer for 10 minutes until sausage is cooked. Remove sausage. Add onion, garlic, carrots, celery, green pepper, tomatoes, tomato sauce, oregano and thyme and cook until vegetables are tender, about 30 minutes. Slice sausage into thin rounds and add to the stock with tortellini. Cook an additional 20 minutes or until tortellini are cooked.

TO SERVE: Ladle into serving bowls and garnish with basil, parsley and a little cheese.

QUICK AND EASY: Use frozen packages of chopped onion, carrot, celery and green pepper.

Nutritional Information per Serving
Calories 250; Calories from Fat 13%; Total Fat 4 g; Saturated Fat less than 1 g;
Cholesterol 50 mg; Sodium 637 mg

JAMBALAYA

This wonderful recipe gets intense flavor from the ham hock and the exciting blend of fresh thyme, peppercorns, clove and cayenne pepper.

Serves: 6

1 smoked ham hock (1 to 1 1/2 pounds)
1 onion, chopped
1 teaspoon olive oil
1/2 cup celery, chopped
2 cloves garlic, minced
2 tablespoons unsalted tomato paste
1 bunch fresh thyme (or 2 tablespoons
   dry thyme)
8 cloves
12 peppercorns
1 teaspoon cayenne pepper
1 3/4 pounds fresh green shrimp, unpeeled and uncooked
1 1/2 cups rice, cooked
2 cups dry white wine
8 ounces Canadian bacon, cubed
1 teaspoon fresh thyme, chopped (or 1/2 teaspoon dry)
2 tablespoons parsley, chopped

Cook ham hock in 3 cups water for 3 hours. Discard hock, strain, chill and defat the stock. Reserve in a large saucepan.

In a large stock pot, saute onion in oil. Add celery and garlic and cook until brown and soft. Add tomato paste and saute until it reaches a deep brown color. Add ham stock to this mixture. Whirl thyme, cloves, peppercorns and cayenne in a blender or coffee mill. Put the mixture into the stock pot.

In a large saucepan, heat 2 pints water to boiling. Add shrimp and allow to boil for 3 minutes. Remove shrimp to ice water. Peel shrimp.

Add rice, wine, Canadian bacon, shrimp, thyme and parsley into the stock pot. Heat, ladle into bowls and serve immediately.

Nutritional Information per Serving
Calories 307; Calories from Fat 15%; Total Fat 5 g; Saturated Fat 2 g;
Cholesterol 170 mg; Sodium 593 mg

MEATLESS CHILI SOUP

If you are in a hurry, try this recipe. It is easy, delicious and an excellent source of fiber.

Serves: 4

1 14-ounce can kidney beans
2 cups salsa *(see recipe for salsa in the Appetizers Chapter)*
1 cup frozen corn

Blend all ingredients in a medium-sized saucepan. Heat to a boil, reduce heat, cover and cook for 6 to 10 minutes, until corn kernels are heated through.

Nutritional Information per Serving
Calories 136; Calories from Fat 4%; Total Fat less than 1 g; Saturated Fat less than 1 g; Cholesterol 0 mg; Sodium 332 mg

GAZPACHO

Gazpacho is the perfect way to enjoy summer garden vegetables. Serve as a first course with crusty bread or with a turkey breast sandwich for lunch. (see color photo, page 23)

Serves: 6

3 large tomatoes, peeled and diced
1 green pepper, seeded and chopped
1 yellow pepper, seeded and chopped
6 scallions, sliced and chopped
1 large cucumber, peeled and chopped
1/2 cup pimiento, chopped
1/3 cup balsamic vinegar
3 cups tomato or vegetable juice
2 cloves garlic, crushed
1/4 cup cilantro, finely chopped
few drops hot pepper sauce (optional)

Whirl 2 tomatoes in blender until chunky smooth. Add to remaining ingredients. Refrigerate for at least 2 hours, season with salt and pepper, garnish and serve.

Nutritional Information per Serving
Calories 67; Calories from Fat 6%; Total Fat less than 1 g; Saturated Fat less than 1 g; Cholesterol 0 mg; Sodium 25 mg

SPLIT PEA SOUP

This smooth soup has real flavor, yet takes less than 2 hours from start to finish. It's loaded with fiber.

Serves: 8

12 ounces split green peas
1 medium onion, chopped
2 carrots, cut into 2-inch pieces
2 ribs celery, cut into 2-inch pieces
2 parsley sprigs
1 clove garlic
1/2 teaspoon sugar
1/8 teaspoon thyme leaves
4 cups chicken stock (homemade or prepared)
8 ounces Canadian bacon, slivered in 1/4 x 1-inch pieces

In a large soup pot, combine the peas with 1 quart water. Bring the mixture to a boil, reduce heat, cover and simmer for 45 minutes. Watch split peas carefully so that they do not boil over. Add the onion, carrots, celery, parsley, garlic, sugar, thyme and chicken stock. Cover and simmer for 1 hour. Cool slightly.

In a food processor or in a blender, puree soup. This should be done in 3 or 4 batches. Return the pea puree to soup pot, heat and garnish with slivered Canadian bacon. Salt and pepper to taste.

Nutritional Information per Serving
Calories 135; Calories from Fat 19%; Total Fat 3 g; Saturated Fat less than 1 g; Cholesterol 16 mg; Sodium 451 mg

TORTILLA SOUP

*This crunchy soup has wonderful flavor and texture.
Use any or all of the 5 toppings!*

Serves: 4

1 teaspoon olive oil
1 small onion, chopped
8 ounces tomato sauce
4 cups chicken stock (homemade or prepared)
8 ounces lean pork tenderloin, ground
1 clove garlic, crushed
1 jalapeno pepper, minced
1/2 teaspoon each chili powder, cumin, paprika
4 ounces chilis, chopped
4 corn tortillas, cut into 1-inch strips

Topping:
1/2 cup fresh cilantro, chopped
1 large tomato, diced
1/2 cup scallions, chopped
1/2 cup cucumber, chopped

In a large stock pot, heat olive oil. Add onions and saute until translucent. Add tomato sauce and reduce until the sauce starts to caramelize on the bottom of the pan. Add chicken stock, stirring in the cooked bits from the bottom of the pan. Add ground tenderloin, jalapeno pepper, spices and chilis and simmer for 20 minutes to cook sausage.

Preheat oven to 350° F. Place tortillas on an ungreased cookie sheet and bake until crisp, about 5 to 7 minutes.

TO SERVE: Ladle soup into large, heated bowls, adding tortilla strips, cilantro, tomatoes, scallions and cucumber toppings.

QUICK AND EASY: Use baked tortilla chips for crisp tortillas. Use prepared salsa for chopped topping.

Nutritional Information per Serving
Calories 222; Calories from Fat 20%; Total Fat 5 g; Saturated Fat 1 g;
Cholesterol 53 mg; Sodium 469 mg

VEGETABLE CHOWDER

Vegetable chowder is slightly different from the other stocks, as the vegetables are not strained. This results in a thick, chowder-type soup. If it is pureed in the blender, it is also a wonderful base for hearty bean and pasta soups such as Golden Lentil Soup with Potatoes (see recipe earlier in this chapter).

Serves: 12

1 teaspoon olive oil
3 large onions, chopped
3 cloves garlic, minced
1 cup fresh or frozen corn
1 cup carrots, sliced
1 cup fresh or frozen green beans
1 cup zucchini, sliced
1 cup tomato, chopped
1 cup fresh mushrooms, sliced

Heat the olive oil in a large stock pot. Add the onion and garlic and cook until well browned. Add the remaining vegetables and 12 cups of water. Heat to boiling, reduce heat, cover, then reduce heat to a simmer. Simmer for 3 hours, adding more water as necessary. Salt and pepper to taste. Cool stock.

Serve as is or puree in 3 or 4 batches in a blender or a food processor.

Nutritional Information per Serving
Calories 47; Calories from Fat 11%; Total Fat less than 1 g; Saturated Fat less than 1 g; Cholesterol 0 mg; Sodium 10 mg

VICHYSSOISE

Make this early on a hot day for a quick and easy lunch or dinner.

Serves: 8

3 cups chicken or vegetable stock (homemade or prepared)
1/2 leek bulb, sliced
3 celery ribs with tops, sliced
2 large red-skin potatoes, cubed with skins
1 cup evaporated skim milk
1/4 teaspoon white pepper

1/4 teaspoon hot sauce
chopped parsley

In a large soup pot, heat the stock with the leek, celery and potatoes. When the mixture boils, reduce heat, cover and simmer for 30 minutes. The potatoes will be very tender. Add the milk, pepper and hot sauce. Salt to taste. Chill for at least 4 hours before serving.

TO SERVE: Place in chilled bowls. Top with freshly ground pepper and chopped parsley.

Nutritional Information per Serving
Calories 74; Calories from Fat 2%; Total Fat less than 1 g; Saturated Fat less than 1 g; Cholesterol 1 mg; Sodium 56 mg

WHITE GAZPACHO

The fragrance of this fresh, cold soup enhances as it chills in the refrigerator. It keeps for 2 days.

Serves: 6

3 cucumbers, peeled
1 clove garlic
3 cups chicken stock (homemade or
   prepared)
3 cups low-fat yogurt
2 tablespoons white vinegar
1/2 cup scallions, sliced
1/2 cup cilantro, chopped
2 tomatoes, chopped

Cut cucumbers into pieces and whirl in blender with garlic and 1 cup chicken stock. Combine with yogurt and vinegar, and salt and pepper to taste.

TO SERVE: Ladle into chilled bowls and top with scallions, cilantro and chopped tomatoes.

Nutritional Information per Serving
Calories 113; Calories from Fat 17%; Total Fat 2 g; Saturated Fat 1 g; Cholesterol 7 mg; Sodium 90 mg

WILD RICE SOUP

This is a velvety, smooth soup with lots of nutty flavor. It's great as a first course or for a light lunch.

Serves: 8

2/3 cup (4 ounces) wild rice
2 medium leeks with greens, chopped
4 large mushrooms, diced
1/4 cup dry white wine
1/4 cup flour
8 cups chicken stock (homemade or prepared)
1 cup evaporated skim milk
3 tablespoons dry sherry
chopped parsley for garnish

Cook rice in 2 cups water until just tender — not mushy — about 45 minutes. Drain well. In a large stock pot, poach leeks and mushrooms in wine until tender. Sprinkle in flour, stirring until thickened (about 2 minutes). Slowly add stock and whisk until well blended. Add rice and season to taste with salt and pepper. Heat thoroughly. Stir in skimmed evaporated milk and sherry. The soup may be refrigerated at this point, and it keeps well. Heat gently, however, being careful not to boil. Garnish with chopped parsley.

Nutritional Information per Serving
Calories 122; Calories from Fat 4%; Total Fat less than 1 g; Saturated Fat less than 1 g;
Cholesterol 1 mg; Sodium 51 mg

BREADS, ROLLS

C H A P T E R • F I V E

If you follow the directions to the letter, you'll have great success with these delicious, truly homemade recipes. Bread making is a most important activity in the kitchen—whether you do it by hand, with your electric mixer or food processor, or with your bread machine. Here are some all-time favorite bread recipes.

& MUFFINS

BAGELS

Bagels take a little time and skill, but these are so worth the effort. You'll love the soft, moist texture and the crisp outer crust! This recipe is very low in fat.

Serves: 12

non-stick cooking spray
1 1/2 cups whole-wheat flour
1 package (5/16-ounce) active dry yeast
2 to 2 1/2 cups all-purpose white flour (divided)
1 1/2 cups very warm water (115° F)
3 tablespoons granulated sugar
1 tablespoon salt
1/2 cup seedless raisins

Spray a large baking sheet with a thick coating of non-stick cooking spray.

Blend whole-wheat flour with yeast and 1 1/2 cups white flour. Combine the warm water, sugar and salt and pour over the flour mixture.

Beat with an electric mixer or with a food processor fitted with dough hook for 1/2 minute. Blend in the remaining flour and knead with the mixer or the food processor (or knead by hand) until the dough is smooth and satiny (4 minutes with electric dough hook; 10 minutes by hand).

Spray a medium-sized bowl with non-stick cooking spray. Place dough in bowl, cover and allow to rise in a warm, draft-free place for 10 minutes. Divide the dough into 12 portions and shape each portion into a smooth ball. Make a hole in the center of each ball and gently shape it into a 1-inch hole for a 4-inch bagel. Place bagel on the prepared baking sheet. Cover and allow to rise in a warm, draft-free place for 20 minutes. Preheat the oven to broil.

Broil the bagels for 5 minutes, 4 inches from the source of heat. Turn the bagels one time, but do not allow them to brown.

Reduce the oven temperature to 375° F. Heat 1 gallon of water to boiling. Cook the bagels in boiling water, 4 to 5 at a time, for 7 minutes, turning once. Drain.

Place the hot bagels on a greased baking sheet. Bake in a 375° F oven for 25 to 30 minutes. When baked, bagels will be deep brown with a crisp outer crust.

Freeze any bagels not eaten in 2 days. To reheat: Defrost, split and toast the bagels in an electric toaster. Or, rinse with water and refresh for a few minutes in a 350° F oven.

Nutritional Information per Serving
Calories 158; Calories from Fat 3%; Total Fat less than 1 g; Saturated Fat 0 g;
Cholesterol 0 mg; Sodium 180 mg

BANANA CINNAMON SWIRLS

These rolls are fragrant and great even without the glaze.

Makes 36 rolls

2 packages (5/16 ounce) active dry yeast
1/2 cup very warm water
1 cup non-fat milk
1/4 cup diet margarine
1/4 cup sugar
1/2 cup low-fat sour cream *(see recipe for*
    low-fat sour cream in the Salads Chapter)
1 teaspoon salt
1 cup oat bran hot cereal
1 egg
1 banana, mashed
4 1/2 to 5 cups flour
1/2 cup brown sugar
1 teaspoon cinnamon
2 tablespoons almonds, sliced
1 tablespoon diet margarine, melted

Add yeast to warm water and allow to stand 10 minutes. Combine milk and margarine and heat to warm. Pour milk into a large mixing bowl and add sugar, sour cream, salt and oat bran. Allow to stand for 5 minutes to soften the oat bran. Add egg, banana and yeast. Mix well.

Blend in flour to form a soft dough. Turn onto a lightly-floured surface and knead until smooth, about 10 minutes. Put dough into an oiled bowl, cover with a damp cloth and allow to rise in a warm place for 1 hour.

Combine brown sugar, cinnamon and sliced almonds.

Knead down dough and turn it onto a lightly-floured surface. Divide into half and allow to rest for 10 minutes. Roll out half of the dough into a 15 x 10 inch rectangle. Brush with half the margarine and sprinkle with half the sugar mixture. Roll in jellyroll style, beginning with the long side. Seal edges. Cut into 1-inch slices and place, cut side down, onto greased baking pans. Repeat with remaining dough. Cover and allow to rise for 45 minutes.

Preheat oven to 375° F. Bake for 16 minutes or until rolls are golden. When the rolls have cooled, glaze with 1 cup confectioners sugar blended with 7 teaspoons milk and 1/4 teaspoon almond extract, if desired.

QUICK AND EASY: You may halve the recipe and mix the first 11 ingredients in a bread machine. Then roll out as directed in the recipe.

Nutritional Information per Serving
Calories 97; Calories from Fat 19%; Total Fat 2 g; Saturated Fat less than 1 g;
Cholesterol 6 mg; Sodium 87 mg

CHEESE GARLIC BREAD

Broil leftover slices for a delicious, low-fat garlic toast.

Makes 1 loaf (12 slices)

1 package (5/16 ounce) active dry yeast
3/4 cup warm water, 115° F
2 tablespoons onion, grated
2 cloves garlic, crushed
1 teaspoon oil
1 1/2 cups all-purpose flour
1/2 cup bread flour
1 teaspoon salt
1/4 cup finely-chopped basil, Italian parsley or curly parsley
1/4 cup parmesan cheese, grated

Allow yeast to soak in warm water for 5 minutes. In a small frying pan, saute onion and garlic in oil until the vegetables are well-browned.

Blend flour with salt. Add yeast mixture, vegetable mixture, herbs and cheese. Knead (by hand or with food processor) until the dough is smooth and satiny (about 10 minutes by hand, 5 minutes by machine). Place in a greased bowl and top with a warm, wet towel. Allow to rise in a warm place for 30 minutes.

Place dough on a well-floured surface and knead down. Roll out to a 8 x 9-inch rectangle. Roll both long edges into the center to form a loaf. Place on a greased baking sheet and allow to rise in a warm place a second time for 30 minutes.

Preheat oven to 375° F. Place bread in oven. Toss 3 to 4 ice cubes into the oven to give the bread a crisp crust. Bake for 20 to 25 minutes, until bread is well-browned.

Nutritional Information per Serving
Calories 89; Calories from Fat 12%; Total Fat 1 g; Saturated Fat less than 1 g;
Cholesterol 2 mg; Sodium 217 mg

CORN BREAD

This corn bread has a chewy texture — perfect for dipping into soups and stews.

Serves: 8

1 tablespoon oil
1 cup cornmeal (white or yellow)
1 cup flour
2 teaspoons baking powder
1/2 teaspoon baking soda
1 teaspoon salt
1 tablespoon honey
1 tablespoon wheat germ
1 egg, lightly beaten
1 cup low-fat buttermilk

Preheat oven to 400° F. Pour the oil into a 9 x 5 x 3-inch bread pan or into a 9-inch round or square cast iron skillet. Place the pan or the skillet into a hot oven and allow it to heat.

Meanwhile, mix the cornmeal with the flour, baking powder, baking soda and salt. Add the honey, wheat germ, egg whites and buttermilk. Stir the mixture until it is just blended. The batter will be thick.

Carefully, pour cornmeal mixture into hot pan. Bake for 15 to 20 minutes or until browned. Remove the hot pan from the oven, cut it into 8 servings and serve the corn bread immediately.

Nutritional Information per Serving
Calories 154; Calories from Fat 19%; Total Fat 3 g; Saturated Fat less than 1 g;
Cholesterol 27 mg; Sodium 492 mg

FOCACCIA (GOURMET PIZZA)

You'll see a lot of variations of Focaccia. This one is light, crusty and flavorful.

Serves: 8

1 package (5/16 ounce) active dry yeast
1/2 cup very warm water
2 1/2 - 3 cups flour
1/4 cup warm water
1 teaspoon olive oil
1/4 cup parmesan cheese, grated
1/4 cup basil, chopped
1 teaspoon salt

Soak yeast in warm water for 5 minutes. Add 1 1/4 cups flour and knead for 5 minutes until flour is well-blended. Allow to rest in a warm place for 15 minutes.

Knead down dough and add remaining water, olive oil, cheese, remaining flour, basil and salt. Mix well, then knead dough to a smooth, elastic consistency. Roll focaccia to fit a 10-inch pizza pan. Bake at 400° F for 25 minutes. Cut into 8 wedges and serve immediately.

Nutritional Information per Serving
Calories 153; Calories from Fat 11%; Total Fat 2 g; Saturated Fat less than 1 g;
Cholesterol 2 mg; Sodium 326 mg

HOT CROSS BUNS

Here's a simple, yet fool-proof recipe for a traditional holiday treat. Easy as they are, you can make them all year.

Serves: 16

1 1/2 cups all-purpose flour
1 1/2 cups whole-wheat flour
1 package (5/16 ounce) active dry yeast
1/4 cup sugar
3/4 teaspoon salt
1/4 teaspoon nutmeg
1/4 teaspoon cinnamon
1 cup low-fat buttermilk
2 tablespoons light margarine
1 egg, beaten
1/3 cup currants
non-stick cooking spray
1 egg white, beaten
1 cup confectioners sugar
2 teaspoons hot non-fat milk

In a mixing bowl or a food processor bowl, blend 1 1/4 cups of the white flour, 1 1/4 cups of the whole-wheat flour, the yeast, sugar, salt, nutmeg and cinnamon. Heat the buttermilk to almost boiling, add the margarine and stir until it melts. Pour the buttermilk mixture into the flour mixture and blend with a wooden spoon or with dough hooks. Add the egg and the currants and knead in enough of the remaining flour to make a dough that is smooth and satiny (about 10 minutes by hand or 5 minutes with a mixer or food processor).

Spray a medium-sized bowl with non-stick cooking spray. Place the dough in the bowl, cover and allow dough to rise in a warm, draft-free place for 20 minutes. Spray a 10 x 10-inch square baking pan with non-stick cooking spray. Place the dough on a cutting board and cut into 16 parts. Form into 16 smooth balls and place in the baking pan. Cover, and allow dough to rise in a warm, draft-free place for 15 minutes. Brush the tops with the egg white.

Preheat oven to 425° F. Bake the Hot Cross Buns for 12 to 15 minutes until evenly browned. Cool the buns in the pan.

TO MAKE ICING: Blend the confectioners sugar and the hot milk into a smooth paste. With the icing, make a cross on top of each cooled Hot Cross Bun.

Nutritional Information per Serving
Calories 144; Calories from Fat 9%; Total Fat 1 g; Saturated Fat less than 1 g;
Cholesterol 14 mg; Sodium 141 mg

ITALIAN BREAD/BAGUETTES/CRUSTY ITALIAN ROLLS

This is a very practical recipe — it makes Italian bread, baguettes, crusty hard rolls, pizza crust and on and on. Add herbs, work with different grains such as cornmeal and just have fun with this recipe.

Serves: 12

1 package (5/16 ounce) active dry yeast
2 cups very warm water, 115° F
2 cups all-purpose flour
1 cup whole-wheat flour
1 cup bread flour
1 teaspoon salt
non-stick cooking spray

Blend yeast with warm water in a small bowl. Allow yeast to grow for 5 minutes. Meanwhile, blend remaining ingredients in a large bowl. Make a well in the middle and add yeast mixture. Knead by hand, by mixer or by bread machine for 5 minutes or until dough is smooth and satiny.

Spray a warm bowl with non-stick cooking spray. Cover dough and place dough in bowl in a draft-free place. Allow to rise for 30 minutes. Remove to a floured board and allow to rest 10 minutes.

FOR ITALIAN BREAD: Divide into 2 pieces. Form into 2 large loaves and place on an oiled baking sheet. Allow to rise for 1 hour. Preheat oven to 425° F. Bake Italian bread loaves for 20 to 25 minutes. For a crisp crust, throw several ice cubes onto the oven floor halfway through the baking cycle.

FOR BAGUETTES: Divide into 4 pieces. With a rolling pin, roll to a length of 14 inches. Turn edges under forming a long, slender baguette and place on an oiled baking sheet. Allow to rise for 1 hour. Preheat oven to 425° F. Bake baguettes for 15 minutes. For a crisp crust, throw several ice cubes onto the oven floor halfway through the baking cycle

FOR HARD ROLLS: Form into 12 balls. Place on prepared baking pan. Allow to rise a second time for 1 hour. Preheat oven to 425° F for 10 minutes. For a crisp crust, throw several ice cubes onto the oven floor halfway through the baking cycle.

Nutritional Information per Serving
Calories 160; Calories from Fat 4%; Total Fat less than 1 g; Saturated Fat less than 1 g; Cholesterol 0 mg; Sodium 179 mg

PIZZA DOUGH

You think up the toppings for this pizza — vegetables, low-fat cottage cheese, tomato sauce, etc. Easy to make, these crusts freeze well before or after baking.

Makes 2 pizzas (6 servings)

1 package (5/16 ounce) active dry yeast
3/4 cup very warm water
2 cups flour
1 teaspoon salt
1 teaspoon sugar

Soak yeast in water for 5 minutes. Add flour, salt and sugar and mix to blend. Knead for 2 to 3 minutes until flour is well-blended. Allow to rest in a warm place for 15 minutes.

Meanwhile, preheat oven to 450° F. Divide pizza dough into 2 portions. Roll each to fit 10-inch pizza pan.

Top with low-fat toppings such as vegetables, low-fat cottage cheese or low-fat mozzarella cheese. Bake for 12 to 14 minutes until bottom of crust is deep brown.

Nutritional Information per Serving
Calories 146; Calories from Fat 2%; Total Fat less than 1 g; Saturated Fat less than 1 g; Cholesterol 0 mg; Sodium 356 mg

SCONES

These scones are popular with children as well as adults.

Serves: 12 regular or 24 mini scones

3 cups all-purpose flour
1/2 cup currants
2 tablespoons granulated sugar
3 teaspoons baking powder
1/2 teaspoon salt
1/2 teaspoon baking soda
1/2 cup low-fat yogurt
12 tablespoons oil
2 large egg whites
2 tablespoons non-fat milk for brushing tops of scones
1 tablespoon granulated sugar for sprinkling tops of scones

Preheat oven to 400° F.

In a large bowl, combine flour with the currants, sugar, baking powder, salt, soda, yogurt, oil and egg whites. Blend until the mixture holds together well.

Place mixture on a pastry board which has been sprinkled lightly with flour. Knead dough lightly, 1/2 to 1 minute. Divide the dough into 12 portions (or 24 mini portions). Smooth each portion into a 2-inch circle with a slightly rounded top. Brush the tops with additional milk and sprinkle with sugar.

Place the scones, 2 inches apart, on an ungreased baking sheet. Bake for 12 minutes for mini scones or 15 minutes for regular scones or until the scones are golden brown. Serve hot.

Nutritional Information per Serving
Calories 164; Calories from Fat 15%; Total Fat 3 g;
Saturated Fat less than 1 g; Cholesterol less
than 1 mg; Sodium 224 mg

APPLESAUCE MUFFINS

Applesauce adds texture and flavor to low-fat foods. Here's a great example.

Serves: 12

non-stick cooking spray
1/2 cup low-fat buttermilk
1 teaspoon baking powder
1 cup unsweetened applesauce
1/4 cup brown sugar, packed
1 tablespoon cinnamon
1 tablespoon oil
1 teaspoon salt
4 large egg whites
1/2 cup apple juice
2 cups all-purpose flour

Preheat oven to 400° F. Prepare 12 muffin tins by spraying with non-stick cooking spray. Blend the buttermilk with the baking powder. Allow this mixture to cure for 5 minutes or until bubbly.

In a large mixing bowl, blend the applesauce, brown sugar, cinnamon, oil, salt, egg whites and apple juice. Mix thoroughly. Fold in the buttermilk.

Pour in the flour a little at a time. Stir until just blended into liquids. Divide into 12 muffin tins. Bake at 400° F for 20 minutes until the muffins are lightly browned and firm to touch. Allow the muffins to cool for 5 minutes before removing from tins. Muffins may be stored in the refrigerator for up to 3 weeks or in the freezer for 3 months. To reheat: Microwave each muffin (high) for 30 seconds or heat in a 350° F oven for 10 minutes.

Nutritional Information per Serving
Calories 120; Calories from Fat 11%; Total Fat 1 g; Saturated Fat less than 1 g;
Cholesterol less than 1 mg; Sodium 236 mg

BLUEBERRY MUFFINS

From mixing bowl to serving platter in 25 minutes! These easy-to-make muffins are great in flavor and low in fat.

Serves: 12

non-stick cooking spray
2 8-ounce cups blueberry-flavored yogurt (1.5% milkfat)
1 teaspoon baking powder
3 large egg whites
1/4 cup granulated sugar
1 tablespoon oil
1/2 cup water
2 cups all-purpose flour

Preheat the oven to 400° F. Prepare the 12 muffin tins by spraying with non-stick cooking spray.

In a medium-sized mixing bowl, blend the blueberry yogurt with the baking powder. Allow this mixture to cure for 5 minutes or until the mixture becomes bubbly.

Blend the egg whites, sugar, oil and water into the yogurt mixture. Fold the flour into this mixture until just moistened.

Divide into the 12 muffin tins. Bake at 400° F for 20 minutes, until the muffins are lightly browned and firm to touch. Remove the muffins from the tins immediately. Muffins may be stored in the refrigerator for up to 3 weeks or in the freezer for 3 months. To reheat: Microwave each muffin (high) for 30 seconds or heat in a 350° F oven for 10 minutes.

Nutritional Information per Serving
Calories 138; Calories from Fat 11%; Total Fat 2 g;
Saturated Fat less than 1 g; Cholesterol 2 mg; Sodium 64 mg

CARROT GINGER MUFFINS

This flavorful muffin will remind you of a moist carrot cake. For sensational flavor, use freshly grated ginger root. Carrot ginger muffins pack well.

Serves: 12

non-stick cooking spray
1 teaspoon baking powder
1 cup low-fat buttermilk
1/4 cup corn syrup
1/2 cup brown sugar, firmly packed
1/2 cup raisins
3 cups grated carrots
1 tablespoon freshly-grated ginger (or 1 teaspoon
    dry ginger spice)
4 large egg whites
1 tablespoon oil
1 cup water
2 cups all-purpose flour

Preheat oven to 400° F. Prepare the 16 muffin tins by spraying with non-stick cooking spray.

Blend the baking powder with the buttermilk. Add the corn syrup, brown sugar, raisins, carrots, ginger, egg whites, oil and water. Stir this mixture well.

Gently fold in the flour a little at a time. Mix until the flour is just moistened.

Divide among the 12 muffin tins. Bake at 400° F for 20 minutes, until muffins are lightly browned and firm to touch. Allow the muffins to cool for 5 minutes before removing from tins. Muffins may be stored in the refrigerator for up to 3 weeks or in the freezer for 3 months. To reheat: Microwave each muffin (high) for 30 seconds or heat in a 350° F oven for 10 minutes.

Nutritional Information per Serving
Calories 177; Calories from Fat 8%; Total Fat 2 g; Saturated Fat less than 1 g;
Cholesterol 1 mg; Sodium 84 mg

RASPBERRY BANANA MUFFINS

This recipe was published in The New York Times, The Chicago Sun, as well as countless other newspapers. These are Mary Ward's signature muffins — and they are delicious.

Serves: 12

non-stick cooking spray
1 cup low-fat buttermilk
1 teaspoon baking powder
1 teaspoon salt
1 tablespoon oil
1/2 cup dark brown sugar, firmly packed
1 very ripe banana, mashed
1 pint fresh raspberries (or 10 ounces frozen raspberries, thawed)
4 large eggs whites, whipped until soft peaks form
2 cups all-purpose flour

Preheat oven to 400° F. Prepare 12 muffin tins by spraying with non-stick cooking spray.

Blend the buttermilk with the baking powder. Allow this mixture to cure for 5 minutes. Blend in the salt, oil, brown sugar, banana and raspberries. Stir until the mixture is well-blended. Fold the raspberry mixture into the egg whites. Gently fold in the flour and mix until just blended with the other ingredients.

Divide this mixture among the 12 muffin tins. Bake at 400° F for 20 minutes, until the muffins are lightly browned and firm to the touch. Allow the muffins to cool for 5 minutes before removing from tins. Muffins may be stored in the refrigerator for up to 3 weeks or in the freezer for 3 months. To reheat: Microwave each muffin (high) for 30 seconds or heat the muffins in a 350° F oven for 10 minutes.

Nutritional Information per Serving
Calories 144; Calories from Fat 10%;
Total Fat 2 g; Saturated Fat less than 1 g;
Cholesterol less than 1 mg; Sodium 239 mg

C H A P T E R · S I X

When it comes to grab-on-the-run foods, vegetable salads have always been small potatoes — deferring to burgers, fries and tacos. According to a recent supermarket survey, quick-to-fix salads (nearly non-existent in 1990) are a $650 million dollar industry.* From Eggplant to Waldorf—from Chicken Sesame to Taco—this chapter will help you become a salad convert.

*From The Plain Dealer, Cleveland, Ohio, July 11, 1995

SALADS

CHICKEN SESAME SALAD

Serves: 4

2 chicken breasts (12 ounces), skinned, boned and marinated for up
   to 3 days in the juice of a lime, 2 crushed garlic cloves, 1/4 cup
   chicken stock and 2 tablespoons tamari or low-sodium soy sauce
2 cups tiny peas, fresh or frozen
1 pound bow-tie pasta
1 bunch scallions, sliced
4 ounces canned pimiento, with liquid
4 ounces sliced water chestnuts, drained
1 tablespoon sesame seeds, toasted
additional tamari or soy sauce, if desired

Poach the chicken in the marinade until just cooked, about 10 minutes. Cool and
slice into chunks, reserving hot liquid.

Cook peas until just tender and cook pasta according to package directions.

To assemble salad, blend chicken breast chunks with peas, pasta, scallions, pimiento
with liquid, water chestnuts and reserved hot marinade. Allow to chill several
hours, then top with sesame seeds. Serve extra tamari or soy sauce on
the side.

Nutritional Information per Serving
Calories 334; Calories from Fat 8%; Total Fat 3 g; Saturated Fat less than 1 g;
Cholesterol 23 mg; Sodium 197 mg

CONFETTI SALAD

*This salad makes a colorful presentation. Make it in advance as it will keep for up
to 4 days.*

Serves: 4

3 scallions, sliced
1 teaspoon marjoram
2 teaspoons granulated sugar

1 tablespoon olive oil
1/4 cup red wine or balsamic vinegar
1 medium zucchini, scrubbed and grated with skin
1 10-ounce package frozen cut corn, thawed
1 medium-sized red pepper, seeded and chopped into 1/2-inch pieces

In a medium-sized bowl, blend the onion, marjoram, granulated sugar, olive oil and vinegar. Add zucchini, corn and red pepper. Chill for at least 1 hour.
Salt and pepper to taste.

Nutritional Information per Serving
Calories 110; Calories from Fat 18%; Total Fat 2 g; Saturated Fat less than 1 g;
Cholesterol 0 mg; Sodium 8 mg

CORN AND BLACK BEAN SALAD

This recipe greatly reduces the fat content of most commercially-prepared bean salads, typically swimming in oil. The touch of olive oil in this recipe is enough, with the flavors mainly coming from the blend of vegetables and herbs.

Serves: 6

1 package (10 ounces) frozen white
   or yellow corn, cooked
1 can (16 ounces) black beans, drained
1 can (4 ounces) mild or hot green
   chilis, minced
1 tablespoon olive oil
1/4 cup cilantro, chopped
4 scallions, minced
sliced radishes and cilantro sprigs for garnish

Blend all ingredients and chill for 1 hour.

TO SERVE: Place on small lettuce cups garnished with sliced radishes and a sprig of cilantro.

Nutritional Information per Serving
Calories 87; Calories from Fat 10%; Total Fat 1 g; Saturated Fat less than 1 g;
Cholesterol 0 mg; Sodium 618 mg

EGGPLANT SALAD

Art Ulene's secret snack food.

Serves: 4

1 large eggplant
1 teaspoon olive oil
1 clove garlic, minced
salt (to taste)
crushed red pepper (to taste)

Preheat oven to 450° F. Put whole eggplant on a pan and bake with skin on until soft (30 to 45 minutes). Remove from oven and cool. Cut off stem and peel away all skin.

Mash the eggplant until extremely fine (by hand or using a food processor). Add olive oil and garlic and mix well. Salt to taste. Sprinkle with crushed red pepper to taste.

Chill in refrigerator. As a salad, serve on lettuce or endive leaves. To use as an appetizer, serve as a dip with vegetable crudite or melba rounds.

Nutritional Information per Serving
Calories 53; Calories from Fat 17%; Total Fat 1 g; Saturated Fat less than 1 g;
Cholesterol 0 mg; Sodium 3 mg

FIFTEEN-BEAN SALAD

This colorful salad is also very flavorful. If you don't have packaged fifteen-bean mix in your market, try blending a few beans of your own. Fifteen-bean mix includes: Great Northern Beans, Pintos, Small Reds, Large Limas, Baby Limas, Black Eyed Peas, Light Red Kidneys, Garbanzos, Michigan Navies, Black Beans, Small Pinks, Small Whites, White Kidneys plus Lentils, Green Split Peas and Whole Green Peas.

With so many different sizes of beans, it is important to give the beans an overnight soak. Our fifteen-bean mixture (after an overnight presoak) cooked in 45 minutes. The beans should be evenly cooked and tender, not mushy.

Serves: 6

12 ounces fifteen-bean mix
1 medium red onion, thinly sliced

1 red pepper, seeded and chopped into 1/2" pieces
2 tablespoons oil
1/2 cup freshly-squeezed lemon juice
  with pulp
1/2 teaspoon Worcestershire sauce
1/4 cup granulated sugar
1 clove garlic, minced
1/3 cup parsley, chopped
lettuce leaves for garnish
lemon slices for garnish

Rinse and sort beans. Place the beans in a medium-sized saucepan, and cover with 4 cups water. Allow to soak overnight.

Drain and rinse beans. Cover with fresh water. Bring to a boil, cover and simmer for 45 minutes to 1 hour, until the beans are just cooked. Make sure beans are covered with 1/2 cup water at all times. Drain and cool. Add the onion and red pepper and toss to mix.

In a small mixing bowl, whisk together the vegetable oil, lemon juice, Worcestershire sauce, sugar and garlic. Toss with cooled bean mix and chopped parsley. Salt and pepper to taste.

Chill for at least 4 hours, preferably overnight, before serving.

TO SERVE: Line a large bowl with lettuce leaves. Arrange salad into the bowl. Garnish with thinly sliced lemon.

Nutritional Information per Serving
Calories 283; Calories from Fat 19%; Total Fat 6 g; Saturated Fat less than 1 g;
Cholesterol 0 mg; Sodium 22 mg

HOT CHICKEN SALAD

Serves: 6

2 cups cooked chicken breast meat, cubed
  (about 1 pound raw)
1 teaspoon salt
2 cups celery, chopped

1 small green pepper, seeded and chopped
1 small onion, chopped
non-stick cooking spray
1 1/2 cups chicken stock (homemade or prepared)
1/4 cup all-purpose flour
1/4 cup cheddar cheese, grated
2 tablespoons almonds, slivered
1 cup non-fat potato chips, crushed

Blend chicken breasts with salt, celery, green pepper and onion. Set aside.

Preheat oven to 350° F. Coat a 9 x 9-inch baking dish with non-stick cooking spray.

In a small saucepan, heat stock. Whisk in flour and cook into a smooth, thickened sauce. Pour over chicken and into prepared dish. Top with grated cheese, almonds and potato chips. Bake for 30 minutes. Serve hot or cold.

Nutritional Information per Serving
Calories 186; Calories from Fat 19%; Total Fat 4 g; Saturated Fat less than 1 g;
Cholesterol 32 mg; Sodium 496 mg

MINTED CITRUS SALAD

Satisfying and light, this salad combines two excellent sources of Vitamin C.
Make sure you include orange pulp in the dressing.

Serves: 2

1/3 cup granulated sugar
1/2 cup water
3 tablespoons fresh mint sprigs (or 1 tablespoon dry mint leaves)
juice of 1 orange, including pulp
1 grapefruit, peeled and cut into 6 slices
2 small oranges, peeled and cut into 4 slices
mint sprigs for garnish

In a small saucepan, combine sugar and water, stir to dissolve sugar. Bring to a boil. Remove from heat and add mint. Allow to cool for 1 hour.

Strain dressing and add orange juice.

Meanwhile, arrange grapefruit and orange slices on 2 plates. Top with 3 to 4 tablespoons dressing and garnish with mint. Refrigerate any remaining dressing for up to 1 week.

Nutritional Information per Serving
Calories 247; Calories from Fat 1%; Total Fat less than 1 g; Saturated Fat less than 1 g; Cholesterol 0 mg; Sodium 2 mg

PAPAYA SALAD

(see color photo, page 28)

Serves: 6

3 papayas, peeled, seeded and sliced
juice of 1 lemon
1 cup non-fat yogurt
1/4 teaspoon thyme
freshly ground black pepper to taste
1/4 teaspoon curry powder
2 bunches watercress

Sprinkle papaya slices with lemon juice. Process the yogurt, thyme, pepper and curry powder briefly in food processor or blender. Place papaya slices on a bed of watercress and drizzle with yogurt dressing.

Nutritional Information per Serving
Calories 55; Calories from Fat 12%; Total Fat less than 1 g; Saturated Fat less than 0 g; Cholesterol 0 mg; Sodium 31 mg

POTATO SALAD

Potato salad is an all-time favorite salad. In place of bacon fat, sour cream and homemade mayonnaise, this recipe uses low-fat French onion dip, yogurt cheese and mustard. This recipe is just about as good as the regular high-fat version.

Serves: 6

6 medium-sized, all-purpose potatoes, about 2 pounds, well-scrubbed
1/4 cup white wine vinegar
1 teaspoon prepared mustard (preferably Dijon)

1/2 cup low-fat French onion chip dip
1/2 cup yogurt cheese *(see recipe in Appetizers Chapter)*
1/2 cup chopped fresh herbs (parsley, basil, oregano,
   and/or chives)
6 scallions, sliced
1 carrot, grated
2 hard-boiled eggs, chopped
3 ribs celery, diced
1 tablespoon dill pickle relish
sliced radishes (optional)
herb sprigs for garnish

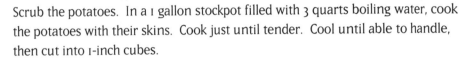

Scrub the potatoes. In a 1 gallon stockpot filled with 3 quarts boiling water, cook the potatoes with their skins. Cook just until tender. Cool until able to handle, then cut into 1-inch cubes.

Blend potatoes with vinegar, onion, mustard, chip dip, yogurt cheese, herbs and scallions and pour over the cooked potatoes to marinate. When this mixture is cooled, add the carrot, eggs, celery and relish. Refrigerate until cold, about 3 hours.

Garnish with radish slices and herb sprigs.

Nutritional Information per Serving
Calories 187; Calories from Fat 16%; Total Fat 3 g; Saturated Fat less than 1 g;
Cholesterol 73 mg; Sodium 574 mg

RICE AND FRUIT SALAD

Here's a salad for people with a sweet tooth. It's beautiful to look at and very crunchy to the taste.

Serves: 6

1 cup raw rice, cook till just tender
1 teaspoon olive oil
3 cups fresh or canned fruit such as halved strawberries, mandarin
   orange segments, fresh pineapple, fresh peaches, fresh pears,
   bananas
1/4 cup granulated sugar
1/2 teaspoon dry mustard
1/2 teaspoon salt
1 tablespoon onion, grated

juice of 4 limes
2 teaspoons fruity olive oil
1/2 teaspoon poppy seeds
2 tablespoons pecan halves

To hot cooked rice, add 1 teaspoon olive oil. Cool. Blend fruit lightly. In a small bowl, whisk together sugar, dry mustard, salt, onion, lime juice, olive oil and poppy seeds. Blend fruit, rice and dressing. Refrigerate.

Meanwhile, toast pecan halves on a cookie sheet in a 325° F oven for 10 minutes. Just before serving, top salad with pecans.

Nutritional Information per Serving
Calories 220; Calories from Fat 20%; Total Fat 5 g; Saturated Fat less than 1 g;
Cholesterol 0 mg; Sodium 191 mg

TABBOULI

The primary ingredient in tabbouli is bulgur wheat which has been steamed and dried then cracked into small pieces. It is used as "rice" in the Middle East and has a distinct nutty flavor.

Serves: 6

1 cup bulgur wheat, soaked in boiling water for 1 hour
2 large tomatoes, skinned, seeded and finely
   chopped
1 cup parsley, finely chopped
2 tablespoons mint, finely chopped
1 bunch scallions, sliced
juice of 3 limes
1 tablespoon fruity olive oil
1 teaspoon salt
1/2 teaspoon cumin
1/4 teaspoon turmeric
mint sprigs and cherry tomato halves for garnish
6 pita rounds

Drain the bulgur well. Add tomatoes, parsley, mint and scallions. Make dressing by combining lime juice, olive oil, salt, cumin and turmeric. The tabbouli salad may be made up to a day in advance to this point.

TO SERVE: Blend bulgur mixture with dressing. Decorate serving bowl or platter with additional sprigs of mint and cherry tomato halves. Serve with pita wedges.

Nutritional Information per Serving
Calories 195; Calories from Fat 14%; Total Fat 3 g; Saturated Fat less than 1 g;
Cholesterol 0 mg; Sodium 795 mg

TACO SALAD

It's surprising how much fat is in fast-food taco salads. The primary ingredients are simple: salad fixings, chili spices, cilantro and tortillas. Try this recipe and you'll never miss the fat!

Serves: 4

4 large flour tortillas
non-stick cooking spray
12 ounces ground turkey breast
2 tablespoons taco seasoning
1 12-ounce can hot chili beans
4 cups lettuce, shredded
2 tomatoes, chopped
2 cups salsa (see salsa recipe in Appetizers Chapter)
1/4 cup low-fat Monterey jack cheese
1/4 cup low-fat yogurt cheese

To make taco shell: Use 2 glass bowls that fit inside each other. Spray both sides of tortilla with non-stick cooking spray. Turn one bowl upside down and place the tortilla on it. Put into microwave. Put other bowl, upside down on top; this will give the taco bowl some form. Microwave on high for 2 minutes. Carefully remove top bowl (it will be hot). Continue to microwave the taco bowl for an additional 3 to 4 minutes until it is crispy and browned. Remove and store in a sealed plastic bag. Allow glass bowls to cool then repeat with other tortillas.

Brown turkey breast meat in a non-stick frying pan. Add taco seasoning and hot chili beans, mashing to make a thick mixture.

To assemble taco salads: Divide meat mixture among 4 shells. Top with lettuce, tomatoes, salsa, Monterey jack cheese and yogurt.

Nutritional Information per Serving
Calories 344; Calories from Fat 18%; Total Fat 7 g; Saturated Fat 2 g;
Cholesterol 58 mg; Sodium 419 mg

TOMATO SALAD

Some people say you can't beat the flavor of a home-grown tomato.
This recipe makes a home-grown tomato taste even better!

Serves: 4

2 tomatoes
freshly grated pepper
1/2 teaspoon fruity olive oil
1 clove garlic, minced
3 tablespoons balsamic vinegar
1 teaspoon fresh basil, chopped
1 teaspoon Worcestershire sauce
thyme sprigs
3/4 teaspoon salt
4 scallions, chopped
1 tablespoon sugar

Slice tomatoes and place in a medium-sized bowl. Combine remaining ingredients
and pour over tomatoes. Refrigerate for 1 hour. Serve on a bed of greens.

Nutritional Information per Serving
Calories 35; Calories from Fat 20%; Total Fat 1 g; Saturated Fat less than 1 g;
Cholesterol 0 mg; Sodium 417 mg

TUNA SALAD

This salad is great in pita sandwiches, tuna melts, stuffed into tomatoes or right out
of the bowl on crackers. You can eliminate the chopped egg if you want to cut fat
just a little more.

Serves: 2

2 cans (3 ounces each) tuna packed in water, undrained
1/4 cup low-fat French onion chip dip
2 tablespoons dill pickle relish
2 scallions, sliced
1 rib celery, diced
1 tablespoon chopped sweet or Jalapeno pepper
1 hard-boiled egg, chopped

2 pita rounds
lettuce and tomato

Blend tuna with chip dip, relish, scallions, celery, pepper and chopped egg.
Stuff into pita rounds and add lettuce and tomato.

Nutritional Information per Serving
Calories 283; Calories from Fat 19%; Total Fat 6 g; Saturated Fat 2 g;
Cholesterol 144 mg; Sodium 803 mg

WALDORF TURKEY SALAD

Traditional Waldorf Salad is laden with heavy salad dressing and walnuts.
This version reduces the fat while preserving the crisp apple flavor!

Serves: 4

1/4 cup low-fat mayonnaise
1/2 cup non-fat yogurt
1 1/2 cups cooked turkey breast, cubed
**   or shredded**
1 tablespoon granulated sugar
4 large, red or yellow delicious
**   apples (about 2 pounds), cored and cubed**
juice of 1 lemon
1 cup celery, chopped
1/2 cup raisins
1/4 cup chopped walnuts, toasted
4 medium-sized lettuce cups

Combine the mayonnaise, yogurt, turkey and granulated sugar.

Toss the apples with the lemon juice to prevent browning. Add the celery and
raisins. Fold the yogurt dressing over apple mixture. Chill for at least 1 hour.
Toast walnuts in the oven at 325° F for 10 minutes.

TO SERVE: Divide turkey mixture among 4 lettuce cups. Top with
toasted walnuts.

Nutritional Information per Serving
Calories 315; Calories from Fat 18%; Total Fat 6 g; Saturated Fat 1 g;
Cholesterol 76 mg; Sodium 188 mg

S A N D W

C H A P T E R · S E V E N

In this chapter, you will find some interesting and delicious sandwich combinations—ranging from the Cajun Chicken Sandwich and the All-American Sloppy Joe to the light and unique Veggie Burger. Any sandwich can be lightened up by using a low- or non-fat bread, such as a pita bread, a tortilla, or other wrapper and using just a touch of meat or cheese. Go heavy on sprouts, lettuce and tomato and light on the salad dressing or mayonnaise.

AVOCADO AND SPROUT SANDWICH

Avocado is full of fat, but it has wonderful texture and flavor. Here, we use just a bit of avocado for a healthy snack or sandwich.

Serves: 1

2 slices whole-grain bread
1/2 teaspoon low-fat mayonnaise
1 slice avocado (1/2 ounce)
2 slices very ripe tomato
1/4 cup sprouts (spicy or mung)
gourmet lettuce (arugula or red tip)
1/4 cucumber, sliced
very thin slices of a red onion
beaumonde seasoning (onion-celery blend found in spice section)

Toast bread. Spread one side with mayonnaise. Layer other ingredients, sprinkling all with beaumonde. Top with other slice of bread. Eat slowly and enjoy.

Nutritional Information per Serving
Calories 233; Calories from Fat 19%; Total Fat 35 g; Saturated Fat less than 1 g;
Cholesterol 1 mg; Sodium 499 mg

BEAN AND CHICKEN BURRITO SUPREME

This recipe is low in fat and full of fiber!

Serves: 6

1 teaspoon oil
1/2 cup onion, sliced
1/2 cup green pepper, sliced
1 clove garlic, crushed
12 ounces chicken breast, ground
1 tablespoon chili powder
1 teaspoon cumin
1 12-ounce can pinto beans
1 cup brown rice, cooked

1/4 cup chilis, hot or mild

6 whole-wheat tortillas

sliced lettuce and chopped tomato for garnish

1 1/2 cups salsa *(you'll find a great recipe for salsa in the Appetizers Chapter)*

1 cup yogurt cheese *(see recipe in Appetizers Chapter)*

In a non-stick frying pan, heat oil. Add onion, pepper, garlic and ground chicken and saute until all pink is gone. Add chili powder, cumin, pinto beans, rice and chilis.

Preheat oven to 350° F. Fill 6 tortillas, each with 1/6 of mixture. Fold sides and roll so that burrito is enclosed. Place on a baking sheet and bake for 10 minutes or until tortilla is crispy.

TO SERVE: Place a little lettuce and tomato on each plate. Top with hot burritos, salsa and cheese.

Nutritional Information per Serving
Calories 288; Calories from Fat 16%; Total Fat 5 g; Saturated Fat less than 1 g;
Cholesterol 18 mg; Sodium 113 mg

CAJUN CHICKEN SANDWICH

Serves: 4

2 teaspoons paprika

a dash to 3/4 teaspoon cayenne pepper
   (depending on desired hotness)

1 teaspoon white pepper

1 teaspoon onion powder

1 teaspoon garlic powder

2 teaspoons dry oregano

2 tablespoons all-purpose flour

4 chicken breasts (1 pound), boned, skinned and
   marinated in the juice of 2 oranges for at least
   2 hours or up to 2 days

4 Kaiser rolls

lettuce and tomato

Preheat oven to 400° F.

Blend spices and flour. Drain chicken leaving it a little wet. Coat breasts evenly with the seasoning mixture. Place on a non-stick baking pan and bake for 12 to 15 minutes until the center is no longer pink. (Or you may grill the chicken on a charcoal grill over medium coals for 10 to 15 minutes.)

TO SERVE: Place on toasted Kaiser rolls and top with lettuce and tomato.

Nutritional Information per Serving
Calories 377; Calories from Fat 5%; Total Fat 34 g; Saturated Fat 1 g;
Cholesterol 34 mg; Sodium 245 mg

CALZONE

Here's a lightened-up version of an Italian favorite.

Serves: 6

1 package (5/16 ounce) active dry yeast
1/2 teaspoon sugar
3 cups all-purpose flour
1 tablespoon oil
1/2 teaspoon salt
non-stick cooking spray
12 ounces low-fat mozzarella cheese
2 ounces prosciutto ham, cut into strips
  (you may substitute Canadian bacon)
3 tablespoons chives, chopped
2 cloves garlic, minced
1 cup pizza sauce for dipping

Combine 1 cup warm water with yeast and sugar in a medium-sized mixing bowl. Allow yeast to soften for 5 minutes. Blend in 1 1/2 cups flour and knead until smooth. Add oil and salt, and gradually blend in remaining flour to make a firm dough. Knead until smooth and satiny.

Spray a large bowl with non-stick cooking spray. Put dough in bowl, turning to coat thoroughly. Cover with plastic wrap, then a damp towel. Allow to rise in a warm, draft-free place for about an hour.

Spray a large baking sheet with non-stick cooking spray. Knead down dough and divide into 6 pieces. On a lightly-floured surface, roll each piece into a 6-inch circle.

Place 1/6 of mozzarella, ham, chives, and garlic on each circle of dough. Moisten edges and fold over to enclose the filling, pressing the edges together.

Place on baking sheet and allow to rise again for about 30 minutes. Preheat oven to 375° F. Bake for 30 to 35 minutes or until the Calzone is browned. Serve warm with pizza sauce.

Nutritional Information per Serving
Calories 324; Calories from Fat 17%; Total Fat 6 g; Saturated Fat 3 g;
Cholesterol 5 mg; Sodium 481 mg

FAMOUS VEGETABLE SANDWICH

The texture and flavor of this rich-tasting spread makes it a delicious lunch choice.

Serves: 4

1/2 pound firm tofu
1/4 cup yogurt cheese
  (see recipe in Appetizers Chapter)
1 tablespoon Dijon mustard
1 tablespoon soy sauce (or 1 tablespoon
  Worcestershire sauce)
1 clove garlic, minced
1 rib celery, chopped
1/2 teaspoon turmeric
1 tablespoon fresh dill, chopped (or 1 teaspoon dried dill)
1/2 cup carrot, grated
3 scallions, minced
4 pita loaves or whole-grain bread
lettuce and tomato

Drain tofu. In a medium-sized bowl, mash the tofu with a fork. Add yogurt cheese, mustard and seasonings. Add vegetables and lightly mix again. Chill. Salt and pepper to taste.

Serve with lettuce and tomato on whole grain bread or in large pita pockets.

Nutritional Information per Serving
Calories 169; Calories from Fat 16%; Total Fat 3 g; Saturated Fat less than 1 g;
Cholesterol less than 1 mg; Sodium 504 mg

ITALIAN BREAD WITH MUSHROOM STUFFING

Serves: 4

1 pound mushrooms (chanterelle, cremini, moonlight or a mixture)
1 teaspoon olive oil
3 scallions, finely sliced
1 tablespoon fresh thyme
4 ounces Canadian bacon, finely chopped
1 cup chicken stock (homemade or prepared)
2 tablespoons cornstarch
1/3 cup yogurt cheese *(see recipe in Appetizers Chapter)*
4 slices (2 inches thick) Italian bread
1 tablespoon fresh thyme
freshly chopped parsley

Separate mushroom tops from stems. Chop stems and slice tops.

Heat oil in a large non-stick saucepan. Add scallions and thyme; saute until scallions are transparent. Add Canadian bacon and the mushroom stems and saute until browned. Next, add mushroom tops and a little water, cover and simmer for 5 minutes until all vegetables are tender.

Meanwhile, in a small saucepan, make a sauce by whisking the cornstarch into the chicken stock. Heat, whisking constantly until sauce thickens. Add yogurt and warm slightly, then add cream sauce to the mushroom sauce and heat thoroughly.

TO SERVE: Make a bread bowl out of the Italian bread slices by removing some of the center. Toast. Place on warmed plates and divide mushrooms among the plates. Sprinkle with thyme and parsley.

Nutritional Information per Serving
Calories 283; Calories from Fat 13%; Total Fat 4 g;
Saturated Fat 1 g; Cholesterol 18 mg; Sodium 745 mg

PITA PIZZA

This pita is quick and easy. Prepared spaghetti sauce is fine when you're short on time, but this recipe is best when you use your own sauce.

Serves: 2

non-stick cooking spray
2 pita bread loaves
1/2 cup non-fat spaghetti sauce
1/4 cup corn, frozen, canned or fresh, cooked and drained
1 small zucchini, scrubbed and grated with skin
2 tablespoons part-skim mozzarella cheese, shredded
1 tablespoon parmesan cheese, grated
freshly ground pepper

Preheat broiler. Spray a cookie sheet with non-stick cooking spray. Place the pitas on the cookie sheet and broil 4 inches from source of heat until both sides are crispy, about 5 minutes.

Reduce the oven temperature to 350° F.

Top each pita with 1/2 of spaghetti sauce, corn and zucchini. Sprinkle with mozzarella and parmesan cheeses. Bake for 20 minutes. The cheeses should be melted and the vegetables hot. Pepper to taste.

Nutritional Information per Serving
Calories 181; Calories from Fat 18%; Total Fat 3 g; Saturated Fat 2 g;
Cholesterol 2 mg; Sodium 348 mg

PITA STUFFS I

This sandwich is an all-time favorite. Try using a wide variety of vegetables but always include onion, garlic and tomato.

Serves: 4

non-stick cooking spray
1/2 teaspoon oil
1 medium-sized onion, sliced
1 clove garlic, minced

1 large tomato, chopped
1 large zucchini, scrubbed and shredded with skin
1 tablespoon fresh basil, chopped (or 1 teaspoon dry basil)
4 pita bread loaves
1 tablespoon parsley, chopped
2 tablespoons parmesan cheese, grated
1/4 cup (2 ounces) part-skim mozzarella cheese, shredded

Preheat oven to 400° F. Spray a baking sheet with non-stick cooking spray.

Heat oil in a medium-sized, non-stick skillet. Add onion and garlic and cook until vegetables are brown. Add tomato, zucchini and basil. Cover and saute vegetables for about 6 minutes, until tender crisp.

Meanwhile, cut the pitas in half. With a slotted spoon, spoon 1/8 of vegetable mixture onto each pita half. Sprinkle with parsley. Blend cheeses, and top hot vegetables with cheese mixture. Place on baking sheet and bake until cheese is melted and bubbly, about 8 to 10 minutes. Salt and pepper to taste.

Nutritional Information per Serving
Calories 238; Calories from Fat 17%; Total Fat 4 g; Saturated Fat less than 1 g;
Cholesterol 17 mg; Sodium 618 mg

PITA STUFFS II

When you're in the mood for a little meat, this is the perfect pita. It's easy to make a single serving.

Serves: 1

1 large whole-wheat pita loaf
1 slice onion
1 slice green pepper
1 slice ripe tomato
1 ounce fat-free ham
1 ounce low-fat mozzarella cheese
shredded basil leaves

Preheat oven to 350° F. Open pita pocket. Stack ingredients in order listed. Close pita, place on an ungreased baking pan and bake for 20 minutes. Serve hot.

Nutritional Information per Serving
Calories 238; Calories from Fat 17%; Total Fat 4 g; Saturated Fat less than 1 g;
Cholesterol 17 mg; Sodium 618 mg

QUESADILLA

Here's a favorite quick sandwich, made with ingredients that are so easy to keep on hand.

Serves: 4

non-stick cooking spray
4 flour tortillas
1/2 cup fresh tomato salsa *(see recipe for salsa in the*
    Appetizers Chapter)
1/2 cup corn, cooked
1/2 cup chili beans
2 tablespoons low-fat Monterey jack cheese,
    shredded

Spray a griddle or large skillet with non-stick cooking spray. Heat to hot.

Spread half of salsa onto each tortilla. Sprinkle with half of corn, half the beans, then half of cheese. Top with second tortilla.

Grill, turning one time, until tortillas are golden brown and filling is hot. Cut into 8 wedges.

Nutritional Information per Serving
Calories 136; Calories from Fat 19%; Total Fat 3 g; Saturated Fat less than 1 g; Cholesterol 5 mg; Sodium 184 mg

SLOPPY JOE

When using flavorful ingredients, it's easy to substitute bulgur wheat for part of the traditional Sloppy Joe ground meat. Bulgur wheat (wheat that has been parboiled) has a soft, grainy consistency that absorbs flavors well.

Serves: 6

1 teaspoon oil
1 medium-sized green pepper, seeded and chopped finely
1 medium-sized onion, cut into small cubes
2 cloves garlic, smashed
1 medium-sized carrot, scraped and chopped
1 rib celery, chopped
1 pound ground turkey breast

1 8-ounce can tomato sauce
1/2 cup bulgur wheat, soaked in boiling water
    for 1 hour
1/4 cup parsley, chopped
1/2 teaspoon Worcestershire sauce
6 Kaiser rolls
thin slices of onion

Heat oil in a non-stick pan. Add pepper, onion, garlic, carrot and celery and cook until vegetables are tender. Push to side and add turkey breast, crumbling it and cooking it until no pink remains.

Add tomato sauce, bulgur wheat, chopped parsley and Worcestershire sauce. Cover and simmer for an additional 20 minutes for flavors to blend.

TO SERVE: Toast buns, spoon on Sloppy Joe and top with thin slices of onion.

Nutritional Information per Serving
Calories 380; Calories from Fat 9%; Total Fat 4 g; Saturated Fat less than 1 g;
Cholesterol 47 mg; Sodium 606 mg

TUNA MELT

If you don't have leftover fresh tuna, use tuna packed in water. Fresh tuna is a little less moist, but more flavorful.

Serves: 2

6 ounces cooked fresh tuna (or water-packed canned tuna, drained)
1/4 cup low-fat cream cheese
1/2 cup peeled cucumber, finely diced
2 scallions, thinly sliced
1 teaspoon Worcestershire sauce
4 slices of crusty Italian bread, about 1 inch thick
2 ounces cheddar cheese, shredded

Flake tuna and blend with cream cheese, cucumber, scallions and Worcestershire sauce. Toast both sides of bread, then pile half the mixture onto each one. Top with cheddar cheese and broil until cheese bubbles.

Nutritional Information per Serving
Calories 183; Calories from Fat 8%; Total Fat 2 g; Saturated Fat less than 1 g;
Cholesterol 26 mg; Sodium 336 mg

TURKEY BURGER

What could be more American than a turkey burger — with burgers being our national favorite food and turkey being native to North America. You'll love the flavor of turkey burgers cooked on the grill.

Serves: 4

1 **pound ground turkey breast**
1/4 **cup green pepper, chopped**
1/4 **cup red pepper, chopped**
1 **egg**
2 **tablespoons seasoned bread crumbs**
1/2 **teaspoon Worcestershire sauce**
4 **hamburger buns, toasted**
lettuce, tomato and onion for topping burgers

Blend turkey breast with peppers, egg, seasoned bread crumbs and Worcestershire sauce. Mix very lightly.

TO GRILL: Grill over charcoal fire about 4 inches away from heat. Or grill under the broiler about 4 inches away from heat. Do not press down with spatula, and turn only one time, about 5 minutes into cooking.

Serve on toasted buns with lettuce, tomato and onion.

Nutritional Information per Serving
Calories 346; Calories from Fat 10%; Total Fat 4 g; Saturated Fat 1 g;
Cholesterol 124 mg; Sodium 470 mg

VEGGIE BURGER WITH CUCUMBER COULIS

This is a very tasty burger—it can be made any size, from giant (6 per recipe) to mini (48 per recipe).

Serves: 6

1 teaspoon oil
1 rib celery, diced
1 large carrot, cubed
1 cup onion, diced
1 cup fresh or frozen peas
1/4 teaspoon red pepper flakes
4 ounces tomato sauce
1/2 cup bulgur wheat soaked in boiling water for 1 hour, then drained
3 large egg whites
1 cup seasoned bread crumbs
non-stick cooking spray
6 hamburger rolls

Cucumber Coulis:
1 large cucumber, chopped
1 stalk celery, chopped
3 tablespoons cilantro
1 tablespoon rice vinegar
1/4 cup onion, chopped

Heat oil in a large non-stick skillet and saute vegetables until tender, 10 to 15 minutes. Transfer to a large bowl and add red pepper flakes, tomato sauce, bulgur wheat, egg whites and bread crumbs. Form into 6 large veggie burgers. Clean out pan, spray with non-stick cooking spray and saute about 5 minutes per side. (Or you may cook them on the grill or under the broiler.)

Meanwhile in a blender, blend coulis ingredients and drain.

TO SERVE: Serve on burger buns, on slices of thick Italian bread or in pita pockets using Cucumber Coulis as garnish.

QUICK AND EASY: Substitute 2 packages (10 ounces) frozen vegetables for celery, carrot, onion, tomato and peas.

Nutritional Information per Serving
Calories 331; Calories from Fat 8%; Total Fat 3 g; Saturated Fat less than 1 g;
Cholesterol 0 mg; Sodium 659 mg

C H A P T E R · E I G H T

This chapter includes recipes for red and white meats. When cooking with red meat, it's important to buy the leanest meat possible and to trim away all visible fat. Prime meats have considerably more fat than choice and are quite a bit more expensive. If the taste is worth it to you, then just serve smaller portions.

Steaks and chops can be a part of a low-fat meal, and you'll see that we've included many traditional meat entrees — such as Chateaubriand, Shish Kebob and Veal Scalloppine. In most cases, the meats in these recipes have been enhanced with vegetables and grains.

MEATS

BEEF BURGUNDY WITH ROSEMARY

Serves: 6

2 pounds lean beef roast (round or bottom round)
slivers of garlic and rosemary
1 rib celery, chopped
3 carrots, chopped
1 cup good-quality Burgundy wine
1 cup beef stock
4 cups cooked rice
sprigs of rosemary for garnish

Tie the beef into an oblong with a diameter of about 5 inches. Make a series of slices about 1/2-inch deep into the meat. Fill those slices with slivers of garlic and rosemary.

Preheat oven to 250° F. Place the meat in a covered baking dish with vegetables, wine and stock; cover and bake, very slowly, for 3 hours.

TO SERVE: Drain Burgundy sauce from the meat and puree it in a blender. Place a serving of rice on each plate, top with slices of beef and the Burgundy puree. Garnish with additional rosemary.

Nutritional Information per Serving
Calories 368; Calories from Fat 19 %; Total Fat 8 g; Saturated Fat 3 g;
Cholesterol 100 mg; Sodium 96 mg

BEEF FAJITAS

The same marinade and preparation method for Beef Fajitas will work equally well with chicken breast or pork tenderloin.

Serves: 8

Marinade:
juice of 2 limes
1/4 cup beef stock
1/2 cup beer
1/4 cup cilantro, chopped

12 ounces beef flank steak
1 large onion, sliced
1 red pepper, sliced
1 green pepper, sliced
8 flour tortillas
2 cups chili beans (hot or mild)

Toppings:
yogurt cheese (*see recipe in Appetizers Chapter*)
salsa (*see recipe in Appetizers Chapter*)
chopped cilantro
sliced green onions
chopped jalapeno peppers

Marinate meat for at least 2 hours or up to 2 days. Broil or grill meat 4 inches from heat until desired degree of doneness is reached, about 5 inches per side for rare, more for medium or well-done.

Meanwhile, using a non-stick pan, poach onion and peppers in a little of the marinade.

TO SERVE: Warm tortillas. Slice meat into thin slices. Place 1/4 cup beans, 1 scoop of pepper mix and a few slices of meat into each tortilla. Top with favorite toppings.

Nutritional Information per Serving
Calories 174; Calories from Fat 20%; Total Fat 4 g; Saturated Fat 1 g;
Cholesterol 21 mg; Sodium 28 mg

BEEF FILLET WITH HOT CAJUN FRIES

Small, tender steaks served in a nest of Cajun Fries, make this a quick and hearty meal.

Serves: 2

2 large baking potatoes
2 tablespoons Cajun seasoning
2 tenderloin steaks (4 ounces each) from the very center of
   the tenderloin
a few gourmet mushrooms, sliced
herb sprigs

Cut potatoes into 1-inch slices and sprinkle with Cajun seasoning. Place on a metal steak plate or heat-proof platter. Heat broiler. Broil potatoes until they are nicely browned and tender, about 10 minutes. The plate will be very hot. Broil or grill steaks until they have reached the desired degree of doneness. Grill mushroom slices for the last few minutes.

TO SERVE: Sizzle steak onto potato platter. Top with mushroom slices.

Nutritional Information per Serving
Calories 460; Calories from Fat 15%; Total Fat 8 g; Saturated Fat 3 g;
Cholesterol 71 mg; Sodium 70 mg

BEEF TIPS WITH NOODLES

If you buy whole beef tenderloin, cut away all fat and membrane, then divide into small steaks. Invariably, the head and the tail of the tenderloin do not make nice steaks. So cut them away and enjoy them in this recipe.

Serves: 4

2 cups beef stock (homemade or prepared)
8 ounces tenderloin tips (or any lean steak cut into 2-inch pieces)
4 cups cooked noodles
chopped parsley for garnish

Heat beef stock. Heat a medium-sized, non-stick frying pan to hot. Place tenderloin tips in it, turning them until they brown to the desired degree of doneness.

TO SERVE: Mix stock with noodles. Top with tenderloin tips and chopped parsley.

Nutritional Information per Serving
Calories 320; Calories from Fat 19%; Total Fat 7 g; Saturated Fat 2 g;
Cholesterol 97 mg; Sodium 42 mg

BRAISED FLANK STEAK WITH PASTA AND TOMATOES

Few recipes allow you to braise flank steak without oil. This one does and it is excellent. In fact, it's essential to the recipe that you not use oil, so follow the directions closely.

Serves: 4

12-ounce package pasta (Orzo or a small soup pasta)
2 cloves garlic, minced

1 large onion, thinly sliced
15-ounce can tomato sauce (salt-free)
3 tablespoons peppercorns
1 flank steak (1 pound)
2 cups dry white wine
5 tablespoons basil, shredded

Cook pasta until al dente (about 8 minutes).
Drain and keep warm.

In a non-stick, medium-sized saucepan, poach garlic and onion in tomato sauce, until onion becomes translucent. Simmer.

Crush peppercorns in coffee mill, processor or with a rolling pin. Rub into both sides of flank steak. In a heavy, non-stick skillet, sear meat until it is deep brown on both sides (5 minutes). Add 1/2 cup wine to deglaze pan. Add remaining wine into the tomato sauce and simmer.

When wine has deglazed pan, pour half of tomato sauce into pan. Top with half of shredded basil, continuing to simmer. Add cooked pasta to remaining tomato sauce. Top with basil.

TO SERVE: Carve meat in thin slices, cutting diagonally across the grain of the meat. Arrange cooked pasta onto serving platter. Top with meat and tomato sauce. Sprinkle with remaining basil.

Nutritional Information per Serving
Calories 344; Calories from Fat 17%; Total Fat 7 g; Saturated Fat 3 g;
Cholesterol 38 mg; Sodium 81 mg

CHATEAUBRIAND

It's become a culinary style to layer entrees with a starchy vegetable and elegant vegetables. This allows the total recipe to be considered "low-fat", but you have to eat the same proportion of potatoes and meat.

Serves: 2

2 large baking potatoes
1/2 cup low-fat yogurt
2 tenderloin steaks (4 ounces each) from the very center of
   the tenderloin

baby vegetables (eggplant, squash, carrots)
herb sprigs

Preheat oven to 350° F. Allow the potatoes to bake until very tender, about
45 minutes to 1 hour. When potatoes have cooled to touch, scoop out the hot flesh,
add yogurt, mash, and then salt and pepper to taste. Divide potatoes into
2 portions and scoop onto a metal steak pan or oven-proof plate and make a well
in the center of the potatoes for the meat.

Heat broiler, then broil potatoes until they are nicely browned and plate is very hot.
Broil or grill steaks until they have reached the desired degree of doneness.
Broil baby vegetables for the last few minutes.

TO SERVE: Place cooked tenderloin in the potato well. Use sprigs of herbs on the
side of the plate with the baby vegetables.

Nutritional Information per Serving
Calories 495; Calories from Fat 16%; Total Fat 9 g; Saturated Fat 3 g;
Cholesterol 75 mg; Sodium 109 mg

RAINBOW STUFFED PEPPERS

With so many beautiful and colorful sweet peppers available, you'll be able to
create a masterpiece of color with this recipe. It is also delicious!

Serves: 6

1 cup bulgur wheat, soaked in boiling water for 1 hour
6 large sweet peppers (green, red, yellow)
12 ounces very lean ground sirloin
1/2 cup onion, chopped
2 cloves garlic, minced
2 large tomatoes, chopped
1 teaspoon ground oregano
1 teaspoon hot sauce
2 teaspoons white Worcestershire sauce
non-stick cooking spray

Cut the tops from the peppers. Discard the seeds and membranes from the interior
of the peppers. Chop enough of the tops to make 1/2 cup. Set aside. Cook the
peppers in boiling water for 3 minutes until they are tender. Drain well.

In a large-sized skillet, brown the ground beef, onion, garlic and chopped pepper until meat is brown and vegetables are tender. Drain fat from pan. Add the tomatoes, oregano, hot sauce and Worcestershire. Simmer for 15 minutes until flavors are well-blended. Remove from heat and add drained bulgur wheat.

Preheat the oven to 350° F. Spray a 9 x 13 inch baking dish with non-stick cooking spray.

Stuff peppers with meat mixture. Place in a baking dish and cover with aluminum foil. Bake, covered, for 30 minutes. Serve immediately.

Nutritional Information per Serving
Calories 154; Calories from Fat 18%; Total Fat 4 g;
Saturated Fat 1 g; Cholesterol 33 mg; Sodium 57 mg

THE BEST BARBECUE SAUCE

This barbecue sauce has lots of ingredients and is really delicious. It keeps well and it can be used for beef, pork, chicken or veal.

Makes: 3 cups, 24 servings (1 ounce each)

1 teaspoon olive oil
1 medium onion, chopped
2 cloves garlic, minced
2 tablespoons white vinegar
1 cup black coffee
1 teaspoon Dutch cocoa
1/2 cup beer
1 cup chili sauce
1/4 cup lite soy sauce
juice and grated peel of 1/2 lemon
2 tablespoons Worcestershire sauce
2 tablespoons steak sauce
few drops hot pepper sauce
1 tablespoon dry mustard
1/4 teaspoon of all or any of the following: celery seed, thyme,
    tumeric, marjoram, paprika, red pepper, ginger
2 tablespoons horseradish
2 bay leaves
2 teaspoons cornstarch

In a medium-sized, non-stick saucepan, heat oil. Saute onion and garlic for 2 minutes. Reduce heat and blend in remaining ingredients, whisking in the cornstarch last. Simmer for 1 hour.

Nutritional Information per Serving
Calories 28; Calories from Fat 9%; Total Fat less than 1 g; Saturated Fat less than 1 g;
Cholesterol 0 mg; Sodium 425

THE BEST BARBECUED PORK

Serve barbecued pork with hominy, which helps to sop up that wonderful barbecue sauce.

Serves: 4

1 pound pork tenderloin, cleaned of all fat and membrane
2 cups THE BEST BARBECUE SAUCE *(see recipe on previous page)*
1 can (16 ounces) white hominy
thin slices of lime for garnish
herb sprigs for garnish

Marinate pork tenderloin in barbecue sauce for at least 2 hours or up to 2 days.

Grill or broil pork tenderloin 4 inches from heat until well-done, turning often (this will take about 25 minutes). Heat remaining barbecue sauce.

TO SERVE: Slice pork into thin slices and put onto warmed plates with a serving of hominy. Pour barbecue sauce over the pork with a little on the hominy. Garnish with thin slices of lime and herb sprigs.

Nutritional Information per Serving
Calories 249; Calories from Fat 18%; Total Fat 5 g; Saturated Fat 1 g;
Cholesterol 6 mg; Sodium 425 mg

PORK STIR FRY

Almost any vegetable can be used in this recipe. Fresh green beans or pea pods work especially well.

Serves: 4

3 tablespoons cornstarch (divided)
2 tablespoon tamari or lite soy sauce (divided)
1 clove garlic, minced
1/2 teaspoon dry mustard
12 ounces pork tenderloin, cleaned and sliced into thin strips
  (or pork stir fry meat)
2 teaspoons oil
1 cup chicken stock (homemade or prepared)
4 cups sliced fresh vegetables, such as green beans cut on the
  diagonal, fresh peas, chopped celery, bamboo shoots, sliced scallions,
  sliced zucchini, sliced sweet pepper
1 cup water chestnuts, sliced and drained
1/2 cup white wine
sliced hot peppers or jalapenos to taste
4 cups steamed brown rice

Combine 1 tablespoon of cornstarch with soy sauce, garlic and mustard.
Coat sliced pork with the mixture.

Heat a large, non-stick frying pan or skillet and add oil. Add pork and stir fry until meat is cooked. Remove pork and add stock. Add vegetables and cook until tender.

Blend Tamari and remaining cornstarch with white wine. Whisk into vegetable mixture, cooking until it thickens. Add pork to heat, then serve over rice.

Nutritional Information per Serving
Calories 441; Calories from Fat 14%; Total Fat 8 g;
Saturated Fat 2 g; Cholesterol 59 mg; Sodium 571 mg

LAMB CURRY

The use of cracked mustard seed, fresh ginger and fresh curry powder gives this traditional recipe a real "kick."

Serves: 4

1 teaspoon olive oil
1/2 teaspoon mustard seed
1 large onion, diced
3 cloves garlic, minced
1 1/2 tablespoons fresh ginger, grated
1 bay leaf
1/4 cup chicken stock (homemade or prepared)
2 to 4 tablespoons good-quality curry powder
12 ounces lean, raw lamb cubes (preferably from the leg of lamb)
1/2 cup low-fat yogurt
3 medium-sized tomatoes, diced
4 cups cooked rice
chopped cilantro for garnish

In a large, non-stick frying pan, heat oil to medium hot. Add mustard seed and heat until cracked.   Add onion and cook until browned. Lower heat, add garlic and ginger and saute for an additional minute. Add bay leaf, chicken stock and curry powder and stir to blend.

Increase heat and add lamb cubes, stirring well to mix with the seasonings. Add yogurt, tomatoes and 1/2 to 1 cup water to make a thick sauce.

Cover and cook, stirring occasionally, until the meat is tender and the gravy, thick.

TO SERVE: Divide rice among 4 plates. Sprinkle with cilantro. Top with curry.

Nutritional Information per Serving
Calories 401; Calories from Fat 19%; Total Fat 9 g; Saturated Fat 3 g;
Cholesterol 58 mg; Sodium 83 mg

SHISH KEBOB

Lamb makes an authentic shish kebob, and the leg of the lamb is lower in fat than many other meats. You can substitute lean pork, chicken or beef.

Serves: 6

1 pound lamb cubes (preferably from the leg), cut into 1-inch cubes
1/2 cup white wine
1/2 cup chicken stock (homemade or prepared)
6 cloves garlic, minced
4 scallions, sliced
2 tablespoons fresh mint, chopped
1 cup non-fat yogurt
6-inch bamboo skewers
2 teaspoons fresh or dry oregano
12 cherry tomatoes
12 button mushrooms
12 small onions, blanched
1 green pepper, cut into 16 pieces
1 zucchini, cut into 16 pieces
12 small new potatoes, blanched

Toss the meat with wine, stock, garlic, scallions and 1 tablespoon mint. Cover and refrigerate for 2 hours or overnight. Blend yogurt with remaining mint.

Preheat grill or broiler. Skewer meat and vegetables onto separate skewers — all meat, all tomato, all potato, etc. Broil or grill 4 inches from heat about 5 minutes per side for lamb and potatoes, less for the vegetables. When meat and vegetables have finished cooking, remove from skewers and place on a large serving platter or bowl. Serve with yogurt.

Nutritional Information per Serving
Calories 278; Calories from Fat 19%; Total Fat 6 g; Saturated Fat 2 g;
Cholesterol 54 mg; Sodium 81 mg

VEAL SCALOPPINE

This is a meal for a hearty appetite. The contrast of crispy veal and soft, flavorful potatoes is delicious.

Serves: 6

12 veal medallions (about 1 1/2 pounds)
1/2 cup flour
1 egg
2 egg whites
1 1/4 cups seasoned, dry bread crumbs
1 1/2 teaspoons dry oregano
1 teaspoon black pepper
2 teaspoons olive oil
12 small red-skin potatoes, boiled and sliced
6 lemon wedges
herb sprigs for garnish

With a meat mallet or the side of a small plate, pound veal to 1/4-inch thick.

Place the flour on a plate. Stir egg and egg whites together in medium-sized bowl.
Blend dry crumbs with oregano and black pepper and put on a plate.
Coat medallions with flour, then egg, then bread crumbs.

Heat a large, non-stick frying pan over medium heat and add the oil.
When the oil is hot, add the veal medallions and cook until golden, about
3 minutes per side.

TO SERVE: Fan potato slices around plate. Top with veal medallions and garnish
with lemon wedges and herb sprigs.

Nutritional Information per Serving
Calories 431; Calories from Fat 19%; Total Fat 9 g; Saturated Fat 2 g;
Cholesterol 132 mg; Sodium 256 mg

C H A P T E R • N I N E

Poultry is growing in popularity, and it's no wonder—it is much leaner than most red and other white meat.

In this chapter, we've used mostly chicken or turkey breast, by far the leanest cuts of fowl.

When using poultry, remove the skin before eating, not before cooking. The skin will seal moisture into the bird while it cooks and there's no evidence that fat from the skin will leach into the meat. The little fat that melts into the drippings may be skimmed.

Buy only ground turkey that says "lean ground turkey breast meat." Look at the nutrition label: Lean ground turkey breast should have between 9 to 12% calories from fat. Otherwise, if the skin has been ground into it, the ground turkey could have nearly as much fat as ground beef. If your meat case does not sell lean ground turkey breast meat, buy a turkey breast and have it skinned and ground at the market.

POULTRY

CHICKEN ENCHILADAS

Cooking chicken in a delicious pepper-onion mixture gives it a rich flavor, with no added fat!

Serves 8

2 teaspoons olive oil
1 onion, chopped
2 cloves garlic, chopped
1 1/2 pounds tomatillos, peeled, washed and quartered
   (or 16-ounce jar salsa verde)
1 jalapeno pepper, chopped and seeded
1 large red onion, sliced
1 large red pepper, seeded and sliced
2 cups chicken stock
1 whole chicken breast (about 1 pound) with skin and bone
1 teaspoon ground cumin
1 teaspoon chili powder
1/4 cup cilantro, shredded
1/4 cup Italian parsley, chopped
3 tablespoons cornstarch
1/2 cup water
8 flour tortillas

In a heavy, non-stick saucepan, heat 1 teaspoon oil. Brown onion and garlic. Add tomatillo, jalapeno and 1 cup water. Cover and simmer for 15 minutes.

In a medium frying pan, heat additional 1 teaspoon olive oil. Add onion and red pepper and allow to brown slowly until they caramelize, about 30 minutes.

Carefully remove the tomatillo mixture to a blender or a food mill. Blend or mill, then strain to remove seeds and heavy skin. Return mixture to saucepan. Divide chicken stock between the saucepan and the frying pan.

Meanwhile, add chicken, cumin, chili powder, cilantro and parsley to the mixture in the skillet. Simmer until chicken is cooked, about 20 minutes. Remove chicken, remove skin, debone, shred and add back to mixture.

Blend cornstarch with 1/2 cup water. Whisk 2/3 of it into the tomatillo mixture. Whisk remainder into the chicken mixture. As the mixture heats and thickens, heat flour tortillas.

TO SERVE: Divide chicken mixture among 8 flour tortillas. Roll, place on plate and top with tomatillo sauce.

Nutritional Information per Serving
Calories 376; Calories from Fat 17%; Total Fat 7 g; Saturated Fat less than 1 g;
Cholesterol 46 mg; Sodium 55 mg

CHICKEN PICCATA WITH SAFFRON RICE

Serves: 4

4 chicken breasts, boned and skinned (about 1 1/2 pounds)
1/4 cup all-purpose flour
1/8 teaspoon red pepper flakes
1 teaspoon oil
1 cup chicken stock (homemade or prepared)
juice of 1 lemon
lemon slices
2 cups rice, cooked with a pinch of saffron

With a meat cleaver or the side of a small plate, pound the chicken breasts until very thin. Blend flour with pepper flakes. Coat chicken breasts with this mixture.

In a non-stick frying pan, heat oil to hot. Cook chicken breasts 3 or 4 minutes per side until golden brown. Remove chicken and keep it warm. Heat stock in frying pan and add lemon juice. Cook until all the browned bits are dissolved and stock is reduced by half.

TO SERVE: Mound rice on a serving plate. Top with chicken, lemon slices and sauce.

Nutritional Information per Serving
Calories 285; Calories from Fat 16%; Total Fat 5 g;
Saturated Fat less than 1 g; Cholesterol 69 mg;
Sodium 68 mg

CHICKEN POT PIE

Almost any vegetable can be substituted for the peas and carrots in this recipe.

Serves: 6

- **2 whole chicken breasts, with skin and bone (about 2 pounds)**
- **3 cups chicken stock (homemade or prepared)**
- **2 onions, diced**
- **2 carrots, chopped**
- **3 ribs celery, sliced**
- **1 10-ounce package frozen peas**
- **1/3 cup cornstarch**
- **2 cups all-purpose flour**
- **2 teaspoons baking powder**
- **1 teaspoon salt**
- **1 egg, beaten**
- **1 tablespoon oil**
- **1 cup cold milk**

In a large soup pot, combine chicken breasts with chicken stock, onions, carrots and celery. Heat to a boil, then gently poach chicken until tender, about 30 minutes. Remove chicken; cool, skin and debone. Slice into 1-inch chunks. Reduce chicken stock to 2 cups, then thicken chicken stock by whisking cornstarch which has been blended with 1/2 cup cold water. Add chicken and peas.

Preheat oven to 400° F. Blend flour with baking powder and salt. Mix egg with oil and milk. Blend the wet ingredients into the dry ingredients until flour is just moistened. Mixture will be sticky. Pour chicken into a 2-quart casserole. Drop biscuit mixture by spoonfuls. Bake until puffed and brown, about 20 to 25 minutes.

Nutritional Information per Serving
Calories 296; Calories from Fat 9%; Total Fat 3 g; Saturated Fat less than 1 g;
Cholesterol 35 mg; Sodium 588 mg

CHICKEN WITH TOMATOES, PEPPERS AND MUSHROOMS

This recipe has intense flavor generated by caramelizing the chicken pieces after they have been coated with tomato paste.

Serves: 4

1 teaspoon olive oil
2 cloves garlic, minced
1/2 cup mushrooms, cut into 1/4-inch pieces
1 teaspoon olive oil
6 ounces tomato paste, canned
2 chicken leg-thigh quarters and 1 whole
　chicken breast, skinned
2 green peppers, cut into 1/2-inch strips
1 red pepper, cut into 1/2-inch strips
1 cup mushrooms, sliced
4 large tomatoes, seeded and chopped
freshly grated black pepper
6 ounces dry white wine
2 tablespoons parsley, chopped
2 tablespoons basil, chopped
2 cups rice, cooked

In a frying pan, heat 1 teaspoon oil until hot. Add garlic and mushrooms and saute until mushrooms are cooked and all oil has been absorbed. Remove to a plate. Heat remaining oil until hot. Place tomato paste onto a plate. Wipe and cover chicken pieces with tomato paste and add to the frying pan. Brown on both sides, caramelizing the tomato paste. This takes about 15 minutes. Add peppers, mushrooms, tomatoes, freshly ground pepper and white wine into the frying pan, cover and allow to simmer for 35 minutes.

Remove chicken pieces and debone. Place chicken back into the sauce with reserved mushroom/garlic mixture. When ready to serve, sprinkle with parsley and basil and serve with rice.

Nutritional Information per Serving
Calories 283; Calories from Fat 17%; Total Fat 5 g; Saturated Fat 1 g;
Cholesterol 34 mg; Sodium 82 mg

BAKED TARRAGON CHICKEN

Delightful to eat, this recipe is sure to be a favorite.
(see color photo, page 25)

Serves: 4

2 whole chicken breasts, skinned and boned
1/4 teaspoon dried tarragon
freshly ground black pepper
1/4 cup chicken broth
1 tablespoon tarragon vinegar
1 teaspoon tomato paste
1 garlic clove, mashed
lettuce, endive and/or other fresh greens
green onion tops

Preheat oven to 375° F. Sprinkle each breast with tarragon and pepper.
Spray non-stick frying pan with non-stick cooking spray. Sear both sides of each
breast, pressing down on the meat with a spatula until browned. Remove from
heat. Transfer chicken to a shallow roasting pan.

In the same frying pan, mix together chicken broth, tomato paste, tarragon vinegar
and garlic, using wooden spoon to stir and scrape bits of chicken from the pan
bottom. Pour over chicken breasts and bake for 25 to 30 minutes, or until juices
run clear when breast is pricked with a fork.

TO SERVE: Arrange lettuce, endive and/or other greens on serving platter.
Place chicken breasts with sauce on lettuce. Garnish with green onion tops.

Nutritional Information per Serving
Calories 263; Calories from Fat 19%; Total Fat 6 g; Saturated Fat 2 g;
Cholesterol 112 mg; Sodium 605 mg

CRISPY "FRIED" CHICKEN

*This "frying" technique can be used to copy the crunch of fried
foods for other entrees such as veal chops, pork chops, catfish,
etc. Vary the spice, but always use a low-fat buttermilk
to marinate.*

Serves: 4

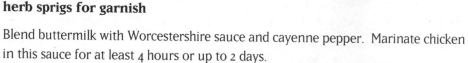

1/2 cup low-fat buttermilk
1 tablespoon Worcestershire sauce
1/4 teaspoon (or less) cayenne pepper
2 whole chicken breasts (1 1/2 pounds),
    boned and skinned
3 cups low-fat crispy-flaked cereal
non-stick cooking spray
herb sprigs for garnish

Blend buttermilk with Worcestershire sauce and cayenne pepper. Marinate chicken
in this sauce for at least 4 hours or up to 2 days.

Preheat oven to 400° F. Spray a baking sheet with non-stick cooking spray.
Crush cereal and place it in a shallow bowl. Coat each chicken piece thoroughly
with cereal flakes. Bake for 25 to 30 minutes until chicken is just tender.

*Nutritional Information per Serving
Calories 154; Calories from Fat 14%; Total Fat 2 g; Saturated Fat less than 1 g;
Cholesterol 52 mg; Sodium 203 mg*

FIESTA CHICKEN

This simple recipe is very attractive and tasty.

Serves: 4

2 whole chicken breasts (about 1 1/2 pounds), boned and skinned
juice of 1 lemon
3 cloves garlic, crushed
1 1/2 cups chicken stock (homemade or prepared)
3/4 cup raw rice
2 ribs celery, finely chopped
1 medium-sized green pepper, seeded and finely chopped

1 medium-sized tomato, seeded and finely chopped
2 scallions, sliced
hot pepper sauce
1 teaspoon oil

Blend chicken breasts with lemon and garlic. Marinate for at least 4 hours or up to 2 days.

Heat stock and cook rice until tender, about 45 minutes. While hot, add celery, peppers, scallions and hot pepper sauce.

In a non-stick frying pan, heat oil. Saute chicken breasts until browned and cooked through, about 30 minutes.

TO SERVE: Cover a medium-sized platter with the rice. Top with chicken pieces.

Nutritional Information per Serving
Calories 216; Calories from Fat 12%; Total Fat 3 g; Saturated Fat less than 1 g; Cholesterol 4 mg; Sodium 28 mg

HONEY ROAST ROSEMARY CHICKEN WITH OVEN-BROWNED POTATOES

When you need a change from chicken breasts, try this favorite recipe. It is unbelievably tender and moist. Make sure some of the marinade drips and coats the oven-browned potatoes.

Serves: 4

1 whole chicken (4 pounds)
1 lime, thinly sliced
4 sprigs rosemary, separated into leaves
4 tablespoons honey
juice of 4 limes
3 large baking potatoes, halved
rosemary and lime pieces for garnish

Preheat oven to 400° F. Remove all visible fat from chicken. Force lime slices and rosemary leaves up under the skin of the chicken and in the cavity. Place chicken and potato halves, cut side up, in a roasting pan. Bake for 20 minutes or until chicken starts to brown. Reduce heat to 350° F and baste the chicken and potatoes with the honey and lime juice mixture. Baste frequently until chicken is deeply glazed and the juices of the thigh run clear when punctured with a fork.

Remove all skin and carve chicken.

TO SERVE: Place chicken pieces and potatoes on a serving platter garnished with additional lime slices and rosemary.

Nutritional Information per Serving
Calories 533; Calories from Fat 19%; Total Fat 11 g; Saturated Fat 3 g;
Cholesterol 138 mg; Sodium 127 mg

MARINATED CHICKEN

Marinating chicken results in a more tender and moist chicken breast.
This is especially important when the chicken is poached and used, for example, in a salad. The following marinades really penetrate and flavor the chicken. These marinades also work very well with pork tenderloin and beef flank steak.

ORANGE WHISKEY MARINADE

Serves: 4

1 cup orange juice
2 tablespoons honey
4 cloves garlic, crushed
crushed pepper flakes
fresh ginger root
2 tablespoons whiskey
4 chicken breasts (about 1 1/2 pounds),
   boned and skinned

Combine ingredients for marinade.

Marinate chicken for at least 4 hours or up to 4 days.

TO COOK: Grill, broil or saute with a little oil in a non-stick frying pan.

Nutritional Information per Serving
Calories 165; Calories from Fat 13%; Total Fat 2 g; Saturated Fat less than 1 g;
Cholesterol 51 mg; Sodium 46 mg

TERIYAKI MARINADE

Serves: 4

1/4 cup lite soy sauce
1/2 cup chicken stock (homemade or prepared)
2 tablespoons dry sherry
1 tablespoon prepared mustard
1 tablespoon brown sugar
juice of 2 lemons or limes
4 chicken breasts (about 1 1/2 pounds), boned and skinned

Combine ingredients for marinade.

Marinate chicken for at least 4 hours or up to 4 days.

TO COOK: Grill, broil or saute with a little oil in a non-stick frying pan.

Nutritional Information per Serving
Calories 134; Calories from Fat 15%; Total Fat 2 g; Saturated Fat less than 1 g;
Cholesterol 51 mg; Sodium 603 mg

QUICK AND EASY TURKEY LOAF

This turkey loaf is much more tasty than meat loaf — it is light and flavorful with a good texture.

Serves: 4

1 cup non-fat milk
1/4 cup tomato paste
2 egg whites
4 slices stale bread
non-stick cooking spray
1 pound turkey breast
1 onion, chopped
1 green or red pepper, seeded and chopped

Blend milk with tomato paste, egg whites and bread. Allow to cure for 30 minutes.

Preheat oven to 350° F. Spray a 9 x 5 x 3-inch loaf pan with non-stick cooking spray. Mix turkey breast meat with onion and pepper. Add tomato mixture and mix well (use clean hands). Pack into loaf pan. Bake for 45 minutes.

Nutritional Information per Serving
Calories 246; Calories from Fat 7%; Total Fat 2 g; Saturated Fat less than 1 g;
Cholesterol 72 mg; Sodium 244 mg

ROAST TURKEY BREAST WITH CORNMEAL STUFFING

Here's a delicious holiday meal that is not devastating to a sensible eating plan.

Serves: 6

1 turkey breast with bone and a full covering of skin
4 pounds fresh sage (or other herb leaves)
1 package (6 ounces) sage stuffing mix
1 cornmeal muffin (2 ounce)
1 small zucchini, shredded
1 medium onion, chopped fine
2 stalks celery, chopped fine
1 egg, slightly beaten
4-5 cups chicken stock (homemade or prepared)
1/3 cup white flour
orange slices, cranberries, herb leaves to
   garnish platter

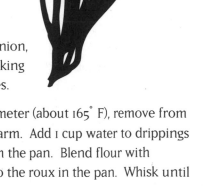

Preheat oven to 350° F. Place turkey breast on a
roasting pan. Loosen skin from turkey breast and
place herb leaves under skin. Roast turkey breast to
medium stage, about 1 hour 30 minutes to 1 hour
45 minutes.

Meanwhile, blend stuffing mix, muffin, zucchini, onion,
celery, egg and 2 cups chicken stock. Place in a baking
dish, cover with foil and bake for 1 hour, 15 minutes.

When turkey tests barely done on a meat thermometer (about 165° F), remove from
oven and place turkey under a foil tent to keep warm. Add 1 cup water to drippings
in pan and heat, scraping all the flavorful bits from the pan. Blend flour with
remaining chicken stock and slowly whisk this into the roux in the pan. Whisk until
smooth and thick, about 5 minutes.

TO SERVE: Remove turkey skin from turkey and slice into 12 thin slices. Place
stuffing on one end of warmed platter with turkey slices on other end. Garnish
platter with orange slices, cranberries and herbs. Serve turkey gravy on the side.

Nutritional Information per Serving
Calories 413; Calories from Fat 9%; Total Fat 4 g; Saturated Fat less than 1 g;
Cholesterol 180 mg; Sodium 637 mg

TURKEY CROQUETTES

This is a recipe that children love to help make — and to eat.

Serves: 4

2 medium baking potatoes
1 pound turkey breast
1 tablespoon Italian parsley, chopped
1 onion, grated
1/2 teaspoon nutmeg
1 egg
2 egg whites
1/4 cup flour
1 tablespoon oil
1/2 cup well-seasoned chicken stock (homemade or prepared)
2 tablespoons cornstarch
1 teaspoon butter
chopped Italian parsley for garnish

Bake potatoes in a 350° F oven until tender, about 45 minutes to an hour. In a non-stick frying pan, brown turkey breast meat. Add parsley and onion and cook until onion is translucent.

Scoop potato flesh out of potatoes and into a large bowl. Sprinkle with nutmeg and mash with a fork. Add cooled turkey meat mixture, egg and egg whites and blend thoroughly (with clean hands). Form 12 oval-shaped croquettes, each about 2 inches long. Coat with flour. Heat oil in non-stick frying pan and brown on both sides, about 5 minutes per side.

Meanwhile, blend stock with cornstarch in a non-stick saucepan. Heat and whisk until thickened. Finish with butter.

TO SERVE: Make a pool of thickened chicken stock on each plate. Sprinkle with Italian parsley and top with 3 hot turkey croquettes.

Nutritional Information per Serving
Calories 302; Calories from Fat 18%; Total Fat 6 g; Saturated Fat 2 g;
Cholesterol 127 mg; Sodium 91 mg

TURKEY TETRAZZINI

This old-favorite recipe is a great way to use leftover turkey breast.

Serves: 6

1/2 cup dry white wine
3/4 pound sliced mushrooms
2 cups chicken stock (homemade or prepared)
3 tablespoons cornstarch
3 cups turkey breast, cubed
1/2 pound noodles, cooked according to package directions
1/2 cup half-and-half
non-stick cooking spray
2 tablespoons parmesan cheese, grated

Preheat oven to 375° F. In a large, non-stick frying pan, heat wine. Add mushrooms and poach until mushrooms are tender, about 5 minutes. Blend cornstarch with chicken stock and add it to the mushroom pan. Begin to heat the stock, whisking as it heats to make a thick sauce. Add turkey and noodles, stirring to distribute all ingredients evenly. Add half-and-half.

Pour mixture into a 2 1/2-quart casserole dish which has been sprayed with non-stick cooking spray. Sprinkle with parmesan cheese and bake for 20 to 25 minutes until heated through and browned.

Nutritional Information per Serving
Calories 341; Calories from Fat 13%; Total Fat 5 g; Saturated Fat 2 g;
Cholesterol 15 mg; Sodium 131 mg

FISH & SH

The biggest problem the American cook has with seafood is over-cooking. The rule of thumb — whether you broil, saute, grill, poach or bake — is 10 minutes cooking time per inch of thickness of the fish. Tiny scallops, then, take only a minute or two, while thick tuna steaks take 10 to 12 minutes.

Fish do have fat; in fact, the fattest fish, smelts, has 62% calories from fat. Other high-fat fishes (30% or more calories from fat) include eel, caviar, orange roughy, mackerel, anchovy, salmon, bass, sturgeon, shark and river catfish, bluefish, mullet, swordfish, and tilefish. Moderately fat fishes (20% to 30% calories from fat) include trout, oysters, mussels and crabmeat. Very lean fishes (with less than 20% calories from fat) include monkfish, water-packed tuna fish, rockfish, snapper, sole, octopus, flounder, farm-grown catfish, clams, crayfish, shrimp, lobster, perch, pollock, grouper, scallops, cod, haddock, surmi fake crabmeat, fresh tuna, and the leanest — pike at only 7% from fat. Many of the recipes in this chapter can be used with several kinds of fish — so experiment.

CAJUN CRABMEAT STUFFED SNAPPER

Fresh snapper is readily available in most market seafood counters.
Haddock or halibut are also good choices for this recipe.

Serves: 4

non-stick cooking spray
1 teaspoon olive oil
1/4 cup onion, minced
1/4 cup celery, chopped
2 tablespoons fresh parsley, chopped
1 garlic clove, minced
1 tablespoon Cajun seasoning
1 tablespoon all-purpose flour
1/2 cup dry white wine
1/2 cup cooked crabmeat, fresh, frozen or canned
4 red snapper fillets, about 7 ounces each
1 teaspoon olive oil
1 tablespoon Cajun seasoning
lemon wedges for garnish
parsley springs for garnish

Preheat oven to 400° F. Spray a cookie sheet with non-stick cooking spray.

Heat the oil and saute the onion, celery, parsley and garlic until the onion is translucent. Mix the Cajun seasoning and flour with white wine. Whisk into the onion mixture, cooking until smooth and thick. Add the crabmeat.

Spread 1/3 cup crabmeat onto each snapper fillet. Wrap into a bundle. Brush with remaining olive oil and coat well with Cajun seasoning. Place on cookie sheet and bake for 10 to 12 minutes. The snapper is ready when the flesh just flakes.
Serve on a heavy platter garnished with lemon and parsley.

Nutritional Information per Serving
Calories 231; Calories from Fat 20%; Total Fat 3 g; Saturated Fat less than 1 g;
Cholesterol 91 mg; Sodium 255 mg

CIOPPINO WITH BRUSCHETTA

This makes a large kettle of a most fragrant stew. Add a pinch of saffron and call it Bouillabaisse — or add cayenne pepper and call it Spicy Cioppino.

Serves: 8

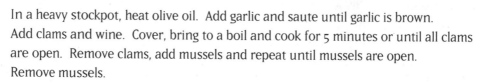

1 teaspoon olive oil
4 cloves garlic, minced
1 pound scrubbed clams
1 cup dry white wine
1 1/2 pounds scrubbed mussels
3 large tomatoes
1/4 cup basil leaves
1 tablespoon olive oil
1 cup chicken stock (homemade or prepared)
1 1/2 pounds cod fillets, cut into 1-inch pieces
1 pound medium shrimp, peeled but raw
8 thick slices Italian bread
4 cloves garlic, sliced

In a heavy stockpot, heat olive oil. Add garlic and saute until garlic is brown. Add clams and wine. Cover, bring to a boil and cook for 5 minutes or until all clams are open. Remove clams, add mussels and repeat until mussels are open. Remove mussels.

Meanwhile, puree tomatoes with basil and olive oil.

Add tomato puree with chicken stock to the broth. Bring to a boil, add cod fillets and simmer for 2 minutes. Add shrimp and simmer for 3 minutes until they are just cooked. Add clams and mussels and heat through.

TO SERVE: Make bruschetta by rubbing Italian bread with garlic slices, then toasting the bread. Place a piece of bruschetta into large, shallow bowl and top with cioppino.

Nutritional Information per Serving
Calories 223; Calories from Fat 14%; Total Fat 3 g; Saturated Fat less than 1 g;
Cholesterol 102 mg; Sodium 314 mg

CRUNCHY CATFISH FILLETS

The mild flavor of fresh, farm-grown catfish is pleasing to most people. A few spices and some cornmeal will add flavor without fat. This is also a good recipe to try on the charcoal grill.

Serves: 2

10 ounces fresh, farm-grown catfish fillets, rinsed
1 cup low-fat buttermilk
1/2 cup yellow cornmeal
1/2 teaspoon freshly ground black pepper
1/2 teaspoon Hungarian paprika
1/4 teaspoon cayenne pepper
non-stick cooking spray

Soak catfish in buttermilk for at least 30 minutes. Combine cornmeal with peppers and paprika.

Heat oven to broil. Spray a broiling pan with non-stick cooking spray. Drain most of the buttermilk from catfish. Roll in cornmeal. Broil for 3 to 4 minutes per side. When fish flakes easily, it is ready to serve.

Nutritional Information per Serving
Calories 301; Calories from Fat 11%; Total Fat 4 g; Saturated Fat 1 g;
Cholesterol 99 mg; Sodium 224 mg

HALIBUT WITH CONFETTI SAUCE

Baking seafood with fresh vegetables makes so much sense — the fresh vegetables moisten and flavor this mild fish without adding fat. (see color photo, page 22)

Serves: 4

4 halibut steaks, about 6 ounces each
juice of 1 lemon
4 scallions, chopped
4 carrots, peeled and shredded
1/4 cup Italian parsley, chopped
3 tablespoons fresh dill, chopped
2 large tomatoes, peeled and chopped
1/2 cup fresh bean sprouts
1 lemon, wedged

Preheat oven to 350° F. Place halibut in baking dish and season with lemon juice, salt and pepper. In a bowl, toss together scallions, carrots, parsley and dill. Spoon over fish. Cover and bake for 20 minutes or until fish flakes with a fork. Garnish with tomato, bean sprouts and lemon wedges.

Nutritional Information per Serving
Calories 235; Calories from Fat 16%; Total Fat 4 g; Saturated Fat less than 1 g;
Cholesterol 54 mg; Sodium 123 mg

POACHED SALMON FILLETS WITH SWEET PEPPER AND ZUCCHINI

This recipe is simple yet beautiful— you'll feel like an artist when you make it.

Serves: 4

2 roasted red peppers
2 tablespoons chicken stock (homemade or prepared)
1 medium-sized zucchini
4 salmon fillets (1 1/2 pounds)
1 onion, cut into thirds
3 tablespoons dry tarragon
3 cups chicken stock (homemade or prepared)
2 tablespoons dry dill
4 sprigs of dill for garnish
4 red-skin potatoes, cooked with skins, sliced

To make red sauce, puree roasted red peppers with 1 tablespoon chicken stock. Salt and pepper to taste.

To make green sauce, steam zucchini for 5 minutes, until soft. Puree with remaining chicken stock. Salt and pepper to taste.

Cook salmon in a heavy frying pan with onion, tarragon, chicken stock and dry dill. Cover, heat and poach gently for about 10 minutes until fish just flakes.

TO SERVE: Put red sauce on one side of plate, green sauce on the other. Put salmon on top of the sauces. Garnish with dill and frame with potato slices.

Nutritional Information per Serving
Calories 384; Calories from Fat 16%; Total Fat 11 g; Saturated Fat 2 g;
Cholesterol 126 mg; Sodium 100 mg

SCALLOP AND LEMON SHRIMP SKEWERS

Scallops and shrimp cook very quickly, so they're a perfect pair in a recipe for the grill.

Serves: 4

1 pound scallops (use bay scallops, if possible)
juice of 2 limes
2 cloves garlic, minced
4 sprigs fresh rosemary
2 teaspoons honey
1/4 cup dry white wine
1 pound jumbo shrimp (about 16) in the shell
juice of 1 lemon
1 teaspoon olive oil
2 tablespoons cilantro, chopped
1/2 cup chicken stock (homemade or prepared)
8 bamboo skewers, about 8 inches long

Marinate scallops in lime juice, garlic, rosemary, honey and wine. Marinate at least 2 hours or up to 12 hours.

Marinate shrimp in lemon juice, olive oil, cilantro and chicken stock. Marinate at least 2 hours or up to 12 hours.

Thread onto 8 skewers, alternating shrimp and scallops. Grill over a hot fire (or broil in the oven), brushing scallops and shrimp with marinade frequently.

TO SERVE: Serve over a bed of lemon couscous or risotto.

Nutritional Information per Serving
Calories 206; Calories from Fat 12%; Total Fat 3 g; Saturated Fat less than 1 g; Cholesterol 168 mg; Sodium 334 mg

SHRIMP WITH ARTICHOKE HEARTS

Serves: 4

1 teaspoon olive oil
2 cups fresh mushrooms, sliced
2 cloves garlic, chopped
bunch of scallions, sliced
3/4 cup dry white wine
2 tablespoons basil, chopped
6 ounces artichoke hearts, packed in water, drained
1 pound shrimp, with shells

Heat oil in a heavy, non-stick frying pan. Add mushrooms and saute until brown. Add garlic, scallions, wine, basil and artichoke hearts and simmer until hot. Add shrimp and cook 4 to 5 minutes until they turn bright pink.

TO SERVE: Serve shrimp unpeeled or peeled with steamed pea pods and rice.

Nutritional Information per Serving
Calories 110; Calories from Fat 18%; Total Fat 2 g; Saturated Fat less than 1 g;
Cholesterol 117 mg; Sodium 142 mg

SHRIMP AND FETA

For this recipe, it's really important to start with a great feta cheese, available in supermarkets or in gourmet cheese stores.

Serves: 6

2 pounds unpeeled, raw shrimp (medium size)
1/4 cup onion, finely chopped
4 large tomatoes, skinned, seeded and chopped
1/2 cup dry white wine
1 tablespoon fresh oregano, chopped (dry is fine)
3 tablespoons parsley, chopped
4 ounces feta cheese, crumbled
6 crusty slices French bread

Shell and devein shrimp, leaving tails on.

In a large, non-stick frying pan, blend onion with tomatoes, wine, oregano and parsley. Cook until the tomatoes form a light puree. Add shrimp and cook just until shrimp turns pink, about 5 minutes. Add feta cheese, and salt and pepper to taste.

TO SERVE: Divide among 6 ramekins and serve with plenty of French bread to sop up the delicious juice.

Nutritional Information per Serving
Calories 244; Calories from Fat 20%; Total Fat 5 g; Saturated Fat 3 g;
Cholesterol 185 mg; Sodium 556 mg

SOLE WITH GREEN BEANS AND BASIL

*Use sole or any mild white fish for this recipe. Cook just until fish flakes —
about 10 minutes.*

Serves: 4

4 sole fillets (about 1 1/2 pounds)
juice of 3 lemons
1 cup dry white wine
2 teaspoons olive oil
1 small onion, chopped
1 carrot, chopped
1 rib celery, chopped
2 cups fresh green beans, cleaned and cut to 1-inch lengths
1/4 cup chopped basil

Marinate sole fillets in the juice of one lemon and 1/3 cup wine.

In a large, non-stick frying pan, heat 1 teaspoon olive oil. Saute onion, carrot and celery until soft. Add 1/3 cup wine and 1/2 cup water and bring to a boil. Reduce sauce by half, strain and reserve liquid.

Add remaining olive oil. Drain marinade from sole and save liquid. Saute sole for 3 minutes. Add remaining wine, cover and simmer for 7 more minutes. Remove fillets and keep warm.

Pour marinade and reserved fish stock into cooking pan. Remove from heat. Puree basil leaves and the combined cooking stock.

Steam green beans until tender.

TO SERVE: Place green beans around the side of a heated plate. Pour a little sauce on the plate and top with a sole fillet.

Nutritional Information per Serving
Calories 243; Calories from Fat 18%; Total Fat 5 g; Saturated Fat less than 1 g; Cholesterol 86 mg; Sodium 154 mg

STIR-FRY HUNAN SHRIMP

Serve over rice or crunchy noodles — the flavors are bold.

Serves: 2

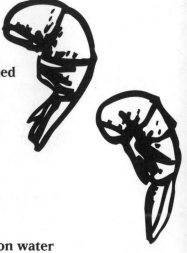

12 ounces large, raw shrimp, peeled and deveined
1 teaspoon fresh ginger, minced
1 clove garlic, minced
1 tablespoon tomato paste
2 teaspoons sugar
juice of 1 lemon
1 teaspoon oil
1 medium onion, chopped
2 scallions, chopped
1 tablespoon cornstarch dissolved in 1 tablespoon water

Blend raw shrimp with ginger, garlic, tomato paste, sugar and lemon juice.

Heat oil in a wok or in a large non-stick frying pan. Add shrimp mixture and cook until shrimp turns pink, about 5 minutes. Remove shrimp.

Add onions and stir fry for 5 minutes. Add cornstarch, stirring to make a smooth sauce. Add shrimp, stirring to coat.

Serve immediately.

Nutritional Information per Serving
Calories 227; Calories from Fat 16%; Total Fat 4 g; Saturated Fat less than 1 g; Cholesterol 277 mg; Sodium 326 mg

STUFFED RAINBOW TROUT

Serves: 6

6 whole small trout, cleaned and boned, 5 to 6 ounces each
non-stick cooking spray
1 cup onions, finely chopped
2 ribs celery, chopped
1/2 cup green peppers, chopped
1 medium zucchini, scrubbed and grated with peel on
2 cloves garlic, minced
1/2 pound tiny cooked shrimp
2 cups fresh bread crumbs
2 egg whites

Wash whole trout and pat dry.

Spray a large, non-stick frying pan with non-stick cooking spray. Add the onions, celery, peppers, zucchini and garlic and cook for 3 minutes. Add the shrimp and bread crumbs and blend well. Mix the egg whites and add to the shrimp mixture. Chill stuffing.

Preheat oven to 350° F. Spray a baking pan with non-stick cooking spray. Stuff each trout cavity with 1/6 of the stuffing. Place the trout on the baking pan and bake for 25 minutes. The stuffing should be hot and the fish should just flake when pricked with a fork. Serve immediately.

Nutritional Information per Serving
Calories 230; Calories from Fat 20%; Total Fat 5 g; Saturated Fat 1 g;
Cholesterol 80 mg; Sodium 141 mg

SWORDFISH STEAK WITH TOMATOES, CAPERS AND BLACK OLIVES

The blend of tomatoes, capers and Greek black olives pleases the eye, and the continental flavor distinguishes this swordfish dish.

Serves: 2

1 medium onion, chopped
2 tomatoes, chopped
2 tablespoons black Greek Calamata olives, pitted and sliced
dash cayenne pepper
1 tablespoon capers
2 tablespoons chopped mint
non-stick cooking spray
2 swordfish steaks, about 12 ounces
2 tablespoons flour
juice of 1 lemon
2 cups cooked risotto
mint sprigs for garnish

Blend onion, tomatoes, black olives, cayenne pepper, capers and mint in a large, non-stick frying pan. Cover and simmer, then remove tomato mixture from frying pan. Clean frying pan. Spray with non-stick cooking spray.

Coat swordfish steaks with flour. Add swordfish steaks and saute until one side is browned. Turn, reduce heat, add tomato mixture, cover and simmer for about 5 more minutes.

TO SERVE: Divide risotto between 2 plates. Top with swordfish steaks and vegetables. Garnish with mint sprigs.

Nutritional Information per Serving
Calories 550; Calories from Fat 18%; Total Fat 11 g; Saturated Fat 2 g;
Cholesterol 66 mg; Sodium 424 mg

TUNA BRUSCHETTA

Serves: 4

1/2 cup low-fat mozzarella cheese, shredded
1 can (3 1/2 ounces) water-packed tuna, drained
4 fresh plum tomatoes, chopped
1 small onion, minced
2 teaspoons parsley, chopped
1 teaspoon oregano, chopped
4 1-inch thick slices Italian bread
1/2 teaspoon olive oil
4 cloves garlic, sliced
cherry tomatoes for garnish
oregano sprigs for garnish

Combine cheese with tuna, tomatoes, onion, parsley and oregano.

Brush bread on both sides with olive oil. Rub bread well with sliced garlic.

Heat a non-stick frying pan. Grill bread until light golden brown. Turn and top each toasted bread slice with 1/4 of the tuna/cheese mixture. Continue to grill until cheese melts and bread is golden brown on the bottom.

Serve garnished with cherry tomatoes and oregano sprigs.

Nutritional Information per Serving
Calories 263; Calories from Fat 20%; Total Fat 6 g; Saturated Fat 3 g;
Cholesterol 26 mg; Sodium 464 mg

WHITE FISH BAKED IN PARCHMENT PAPER

It's fun to watch this recipe cook — the parchment paper puffs and swells as the fish cooks. Use any white fish such as sole, flounder, perch, pollock or snapper for this recipe. The sauce in this meal is incredible!

Serves: 2

2 large squares (12 x 12-inch) parchment paper (or aluminum foil)
4 small white fish fillets, about 12 ounces
2 medium-sized potatoes, sliced thin
2 plum tomatoes, peeled and chopped
4 Greek Calamata olives, sliced and pitted
1/4 cup Italian parsley, chopped
1/4 cup dry white wine
juice of 1 lemon
1 egg white

Preheat oven to 400° F.

Place parchment paper on working surface. Top with 2 small fish fillets. Cover with half of potato, tomatoes, olives, parsley, salt and pepper. Sprinkle with half of wine and lemon juice. Repeat with second parchment square.

Pleat and fold parchment paper to ensure that all edges are sealed. After sealing, rub a little egg white on folds and pleats. During baking, this will act as glue.

Place parchment packages on a baking tray and into the oven for 25 minutes.

TO SERVE: Place parchment package on each plate. Open and enjoy.

Nutritional Information per Serving
Calories 345; Calories from Fat 8%; Total Fat 3 g; Saturated Fat less than 1 g;
Cholesterol 152 mg; Sodium 201 mg

WHITE FISH WITH PESTO

Pesto presents a great alternative dressing for seafood. This recipe is great with any of the lean fishes, including snapper, sole, rockfish, flounder and haddock.

Serves: 2

2 white fish fillets, about 12 ounces
juice of 1 lemon
basil sprigs for garnish

Pesto Sauce:
1 1/2 teaspoons fruity olive oil
1 teaspoon chicken stock
2 cloves garlic, peeled and sliced
1 1/2 teaspoons pine nuts, toasted
1/4 cup basil leaves
1 1/2 teaspoons Italian parsley

Preheat oven to 450° F. Blend pesto ingredients until smooth. Place fillets in an oven-proof baking dish. Squeeze lemon juice over fish. Spread pesto over fish.

Bake until fish just flakes, about 10 minutes.

TO SERVE: Place on heated plates with sprigs of basil for garnish.

Nutritional Information per Serving
Calories 197; Calories from Fat 17%; Total Fat 4 g;
Saturated Fat less than 1 g; Cholesterol 152 mg; Sodium 118 mg

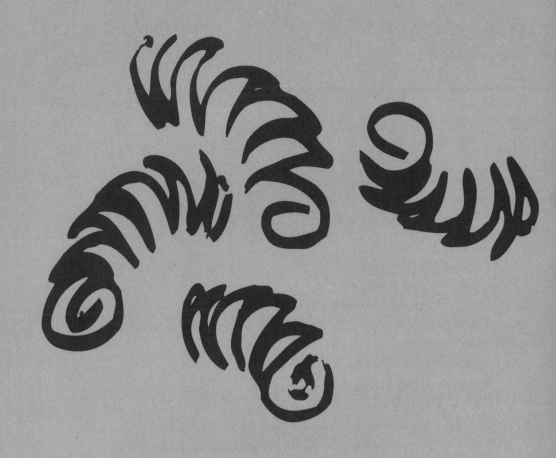

CHAPTER · ELEVEN

Pasta dishes are as diverse as the shapes and sizes of today's pasta. It is difficult to think of another food that can look as appealing, taste as good and please as many different palates as pasta.

Try these recipes and see how pasta provides the perfect meal — whether with seafood or vegetables, meat or cheese, pasta is a great choice for today's busy cook.

P A S T A

BOW-TIE PASTA WITH ZUCCHINI ASIAGO

The flavor of this sauce comes from the intense stewing of the squash.
The aroma of this sauce is wonderful.

Serves: 4

1 teaspoon oil
1 medium onion, cubed
2 cloves garlic, minced
1 teaspoon (or less) hot pepper flakes
2 zucchini, sliced and halved into half-moons
2 yellow squash, sliced and halved into half-moons
1/4 cup parsley, chopped
8 ounces bow-tie pasta, cooked according to package directions
1/4 cup asiago (or other hard Italian cheese), grated
parsley sprigs for garnish

In a heavy, non-stick frying pan, heat oil. Add onion and garlic and saute until translucent. Add zucchini and yellow squash and saute until they just start to brown. Lower heat, cover pan and cook for 30 minutes, until zucchini stews and makes a thick sauce. Add water if sauce seems to be sticking to the pan. Puree in a blender or food processor. Add parsley and heat. Salt and pepper to taste.

TO SERVE: Divide cooked bow-ties among four plates. Top with zucchini sauce and asiago cheese. Garnish with additional parsley sprigs.

Nutritional Information per Serving
Calories 303; Calories from Fat 18%;
Total Fat 6 g; Saturated Fat 3 g;
Cholesterol 15 mg; Sodium 463 mg

CAPELLINI LA CHECCA

The title of this recipe means "a pasta for the common man." Again, simplicity rules here with the secret being the tomato water and the way it is incorporated into the capellini, or angel hair, pasta.

Serves: 6

1 tablespoon butter
10 Roma tomatoes (or a 29-ounce can Roma tomatoes)
1/4 cup basil leaves, chopped
1 teaspoon salt
1 teaspoon pepper, freshly grated
1 pound capellini (angel hair pasta)
2 cloves garlic, chopped
1 tablespoon olive oil
3 tablespoons Romano cheese

Chop tomatoes into 1/4-inch pieces. Blend with basil leaves, salt and pepper. Allow to stand for at least 1 hour or preferably, 4 to 6 hours, to allow the tomatoes time to "weep" and to form tomato water. .

In a large soup pot, heat 4 quarts water to boiling. Meanwhile, in a small, non-stick frying pan, saute garlic in olive oil. Drain tomato water from tomato and basil mixture into a large bowl and, carefully, add garlic olive oil to mixture.

When water boils, add capellini and swirl it with a long fork for 2 minutes. Drain capellini and, with tongs, dip pasta into the tomato water. Continue to dip and swirl the capellini until all of the tomato water has been absorbed.

TO SERVE: Divide capellini among 4 large bowls and top with Romano cheese and the tomato-basil dressing.

Nutritional Information per Serving
Calories 372; Calories from Fat 15%; Total Fat 6 g; Saturated Fat 2 g;
Cholesterol 7 mg; Sodium 465 mg

GNOCCHI WITH PROVOLONE

The secret to this recipe lies in how to blend the flour into the potatoes to achieve just the right consistency.

Serves: 4

3 large baking potatoes (about 2 pounds)
1 to 1 1/4 cups all-purpose flour, sifted
1 teaspoon salt
non-stick cooking spray

6 ounces provolone cheese, sliced
freshly grated black pepper

Preheat oven to 375° F. Prick potatoes and bake for
1 hour or until tender. Remove, cool slightly and
scoop out flesh. Mash with a fork. Cool
thoroughly, allowing potatoes to dry out. Stir in
only enough flour and salt so that the dough is smooth
and elastic (the less flour, the more tender the gnocchi). Roll into small, 6-inch long
x 1-inch diameter cylinders and cut into 1/2-inch disks.

In a large soup pot, heat 4 quarts water. Boil gnocchi for 5 minutes, until tender.

Spray a 9 x 9-inch square baking dish or pan with non- stick cooking spray. Preheat
oven to 475° F. Arrange gnocci in 2 layers with slices of cheese between. Grind
black pepper over top and bake for 20 minutes or until golden brown.

Nutritional Information per Serving
Calories 360; Calories from Fat 16%; Total Fat 6 g; Saturated Fat 7 g;
Cholesterol 26 mg; Sodium 750 mg

LINGUINE WITH SHRIMP AND ARUGULA

This recipe offers a fiery pasta sauce with the surprise combination of tart arugula
and tender shrimp.

Serves: 4

1 teaspoon olive oil
1 small onion, chopped
1 clove garlic, halved
4 medium-sized, very ripe tomatoes, quartered
   (or 1 29-ounce can crushed tomatoes)
1/4 teaspoon (or less) cayenne pepper
2 cups arugula lettuce (if not available use spinach)
2 pounds medium-sized shrimp, in shell
1/4 cup parsley
8 ounces linguine, cooked al dente (2 minutes less than
   package directions)

In a small, non-stick sauce pan, heat olive oil. Add onion and garlic and saute until
translucent. Puree tomatoes in a processor with onion and garlic mixture.

Return puree to sauce pan, adding cayenne pepper and 1 1/2 cups arugula.

Shell and devein shrimp. Add to tomato mixture with parsley. Cook just until shrimp turn pink, about 4 minutes.

When ready to serve, stir al dente pasta into tomato sauce and allow it to absorb flavors and finish cooking. Just before serving, add remaining 1/2 cup arugula.

Nutritional Information per Serving
Calories 196; Calories from Fat 13%; Total Fat 3 g; Saturated Fat less than 1 g;
Cholesterol 196 mg; Sodium 239 mg

LINGUINE WITH WHITE CLAM SAUCE

Try this recipe for a quick and easy dinner.

Serves: 4

2 cans (6 1/2 ounces each) chopped clams
1 teaspoon olive oil
4 cloves garlic, minced
1 cup chicken stock (homemade
   or prepared)
1/2 cup dry white wine
1/4 cup parsley, chopped
8 ounces linguine, cooked according to
   package directions
4 tablespoons basil, shredded
basil leaves for garnish
1 tablespoon fontina cheese, grated

Drain clams, saving liquid.

Heat olive oil in a large, non-stick frying pan. Add garlic and cook until just light brown. Add reserved liquid, chicken stock, white wine and parsley and heat to a boil. Boil and reduce broth to about 1 cup. Add clams.

TO SERVE: Place linguine on a large platter. Sprinkle basil over linguine and top with hot sauce. Top with grated cheese. Garnish with additional basil leaves.

Nutritional Information per Serving
Calories 297; Calories from Fat 16%; Total Fat 5 g; Saturated Fat 2 g;
Cholesterol 66 mg; Sodium 111 mg

MACARONI AND CHEESE

This recipe especially appeals to children.

Serves: 6

1 pound macaroni
1 cup low-fat buttermilk
2 cups non-fat cottage cheese
non-stick cooking spray
1 1/2 cups low-fat cheddar cheese, sliced
1/4 cup parmesan cheese, grated

Cook macaroni according to package directions. While macaroni cooks, blend together buttermilk and cheddar cheese.

Spray a 9 x 13 x 2-inch casserole dish with non-stick cooking spray. Preheat oven to 350° F. Return cooked and drained macaroni to cooking pan. Blend with cheddar and mozzarella cheese until cheese has melted. Add buttermilk mixture and stir through. Pour into prepared casserole dish, top with parmesan cheese and bake until browned and bubbly, about 30 minutes.

Nutritional Information per Serving
Calories 451; Calories from Fat 18%; Total Fat 9 g; Saturated Fat 3 g;
Cholesterol 16 mg; Sodium 418 mg

OPEN RAVIOLIS WITH SCALLOPS

These little pasta sandwiches take a little work, but are worth it. If you don't have a pasta rolling machine, roll the pasta out by hand.

Serves: 4

For White Pasta:
1 cup all-purpose flour
1 egg
2 tablespoons water

For Green Pasta:
1 cup all-purpose flour
2 tablespoons spinach puree (or you may use baby food spinach)
1 egg

Scallop Filling:
1 teaspoon butter
1 pound small scallops
1 cup dry wine
1/4 cup half-and-half
1 tablespoon cornstarch
white pepper
basil leaves

TO MAKE WHITE PASTA: Blend flour with egg and a little water. Knead by hand or by food processor for 5 minutes. Wrap with plastic wrap and allow to rest for 30 minutes.

TO MAKE GREEN PASTA: Blend flour with spinach and egg. Knead by hand or by food processor for 5 minutes. Wrap with plastic wrap and allow to rest for 30 minutes.

With rolling machine or with a rolling pin, roll out both pastas until thin and cut into 3 x 4-inch pieces. You may need a little additional flour if the dough is sticky. There should be 8 white and 8 green rectangles. Cook sheets in boiling water for 4 minutes and drain.

In a large, non-stick frying pan, heat butter to medium. Add scallops and gently saute until just cooked, about 2 minutes. Add wine. Blend half-and-half with cornstarch, and whisk mixture into the wine to thicken slightly.

TO SERVE: Place 2 pieces of green pasta on a plate. Top with 1/4 of the filling and a dash of white pepper. Top with white pasta, putting a basil leaf on each piece.

Nutritional Information per Serving
Calories 384; Calories from Fat 16%; Total Fat 7 g; Saturated Fat 3 g;
Cholesterol 152 mg; Sodium 236 mg

PASTA E FAGIOLI

This favorite Italian soup is a meal in itself.

Serves: 4

1 tablespoon olive oil
1 large onion, chopped
2 cloves garlic, minced
2 ribs celery, sliced

2 carrots, chopped

3 sprigs fresh thyme (or 1 tablespoon dry)

2 tablespoons fresh oregano, chopped (or 1 teaspoon dry)

1 can (28 ounces) crushed Italian tomatoes, with liquid

3 cups chicken stock (homemade or prepared)

8 ounces navy beans, soaked and cooked according to
    package directions

2 cup rigatoni, cooked

1/2 cup basil leaves or escarole, shredded

In a large, non-stick soup pot, heat olive oil. Add onion, garlic, celery and carrots and saute until very tender. Add thyme sprigs, chopped oregano, tomatoes and stock; cover and simmer for 1 hour.

TO SERVE: Add beans and rigatoni and heat through. Garnish with sliced basil or shredded escarole.

Nutritional Information per Serving
Calories 336; Calories from Fat 14%; Total Fat 5 g; Saturated Fat less than 1 g;
Cholesterol 38 mg; Sodium 376 mg

PASTA WITH MEAT SAUCE

This versatile sauce may be used for pasta, for pizza or as an all-purpose tomato sauce.

Serves: 10

2 teaspoons olive oil

4 cloves garlic, minced

1 large onion, chopped

1 pound lean ground beef

2 16-ounce cans tomato sauce

1 28-ounce can crushed Italian tomatoes

1/2 cup dry red wine

2 tablespoons fresh oregano or marjoram,
    chopped (or 2 teaspoons dry)

1/4 cup thyme sprigs (or 1 tablespoon dry thyme)

1/2 cup Italian parsley, chopped

hot red pepper flakes (optional)

1 1/2 pounds pasta, cooked

Heat oil in a very large, non-stick frying pan. Add garlic and onion and saute until transparent. Add ground beef and cook until it has lost all red color. Drain any fat from pan.

Add tomato sauce, tomatoes, red wine, herbs and hot pepper flakes.

Serve over pasta or use as an ingredient for other dishes.

Nutritional Information per Serving
Calories 355; Calories from Fat 11%; Total Fat 4 g;
Saturated Fat 1 g; Cholesterol 29 mg; Sodium 175 mg

PASTA WITH SPINACH AND CHICKEN

This recipe is ready in 45 minutes.

Serves: 4

1 teaspoon red pepper flakes
1 teaspoon olive oil
2 cloves garlic, minced
1 pound fresh spinach, washed and stemmed
8 plum tomatoes, chopped (or use 2 cups canned, crushed tomatoes)
1 whole chicken breast, with skin, about 1 pound
4 cups cooked pasta
1/2 cup fresh basil, chopped

In a heavy, non-stick soup pot, brown red pepper flakes in hot oil. Add garlic, stirring so that it does not burn. Add spinach in batches, cooking it down. Add tomatoes and chicken breast. Cover and simmer for 30 minutes. Remove chicken breast. Skin, remove bones, slice and add back to spinach-tomato mixture.

TO SERVE: Stir cooked pasta into spinach-tomato sauce with fresh basil. Serve on a large, heated platter garnished with additional basil.

Nutritional Information per Serving
Calories 266; Calories from Fat 17%; Total Fat 5 g;
Saturated Fat 1 g; Cholesterol 69 mg; Sodium 212 mg

PASTA WITH FRESH TOMATOES

Fresh, home-grown tomatoes make this recipe superior to any fresh sauce. In a pinch, canned tomatoes may be substituted. (see color photo, page 27)

Serves: 4

**4 large, ripe tomatoes, diced
  (or a 28-ounce can crushed tomatoes)
4 cloves garlic, sliced
2 tablespoons olive oil
1/2 cup basil leaves
2 tablespoons Italian parsley
8 ounces tubular pasta, such as rigatoni or penne, cooked
herb sprigs for garnish**

Place all ingredients in a blender cup. Pulse several times or until sauce is smooth. Salt and pepper to taste.

Heat or serve at room temperature over hot pasta. Garnish with additional herb sprigs.

Nutritional Information per Serving
Calories 283; Calories from Fat 15%; Total Fat 5 g; Saturated Fat less than 1 g; Cholesterol 0 mg; Sodium 21 mg

PASTA WITH TOMATOES, MOZZARELLA AND BASIL

Here's a wonderful way to dress a fresh pasta sauce.

Serves: 4

**8 ounces pasta, cooked
2-ounces fresh (or baby) mozzarella cheese, cut into wedges
2 cups fresh tomato sauce
  (see previous recipe, Pasta With Fresh Tomatoes)
shredded basil, for garnish**

In a large bowl, blend hot pasta with fresh mozzarella cheese. Allow pasta to rest as cheese melts.

TO SERVE: Nap each plate with 1/2 cup fresh tomato sauce. Divide pasta among plates. Garnish with shredded basil.

Nutritional Information per Serving
Calories 292; Calories from Fat 18%; Total Fat 6 g; Saturated Fat 2 g; Cholesterol 7 mg;
Sodium 53 mg

RIGATONI IN FRESH TOMATO SAUCE WITH SHELLFISH

Be careful to really scrub the shellfish so that sand doesn't get into the sauce.

Serves: 8

1 dozen mussels, scrubbed and washed
1 dozen clams, scrubbed and washed
2 cups fresh tomato sauce *(see recipe, Pasta With Fresh Tomatoes,*
    earlier in this chapter)
1/2 pound mushrooms, sliced
1 cup dry white wine
1/2 pound bay or sea scallops
1 pound rigatoni, cooked according to package directions

Scrub clams and mussels, removing beards from mussels and discarding any clams or mussels that have opened. Soak for 1 hour in a solution of 1 gallon water with 2 tablespoons cornmeal to remove any excess sand.

Heat fresh tomato sauce. Add mushrooms, clams, mussels and cook until shellfish open, about 5 minutes. Remove shellfish and keep them warm.

Add white wine, heat and add scallops. Allow them to cook until just tender, about 5 to 8 minutes depending on their size.

TO SERVE: Portion rigatoni onto plates. Top with clams, mussels and the scallop sauce.

Nutritional Information per Serving
Calories 453; Calories from Fat 13%; Total Fat 7 g;
Saturated Fat less than 1 g; Cholesterol 122 mg;
Sodium 612 mg

SHELLS STUFFED WITH EGGPLANT PARMESAN

Easy to make, Eggplant Parmesan makes a delicious stuffing for these tender shells.

Serves: 8

2 small eggplants (or 1 large), about 2 pounds
1/2 cup seasoned bread crumbs
1/4 cup parmesan cheese, grated
2 tablespoons basil, shredded
3 cloves garlic, minced
16 large stuffing shells (about 12 ounces), cooked half the time
    directed on package
1/4 cup low-fat mozzarella cheese, shredded
non-stick cooking spray
2 cups fresh tomato sauce*(see recipe, Pasta With Fresh Tomatoes,
    earlier in this chapter)*
basil leaves for garnish

Heat oven to 400° F. Bake eggplant until very soft inside, about 30 minutes for small, 45 minutes for large. Cool. Scoop interior into a medium-sized bowl. There should be about 4 cups. Blend with bread crumbs, parmesan cheese, basil and garlic. Divide among shells. Spray a baking dish with non-stick cooking spray. Layer shells into the dish, cover with aluminum foil and return to the oven to heat for about 15 minutes.

TO SERVE: Nap each plate with 1/4 cup sauce, 2 shells and basil as a garnish.

Nutritional Information per Serving
Calories 265; Calories from Fat 15%; Total Fat 4 g; Saturated Fat 1 g;
Cholesterol 3 mg; Sodium 159 mg

TORTELLINI IN FRESH TOMATO SAUCE

Any stuffing will work in these tortellini — a little piece of sharp cheese, a little bit of meatball or this wonderful stuffing.

Serves: 6

8 ounces ground turkey breast
5 sage leaves, minced
2 ounces Canadian bacon, minced
1 slice white bread soaked in milk
3 cups all-purpose flour
2 eggs
1/2 teaspoon salt
2 cups fresh tomato sauce (see recipe, Pasta With Fresh Tomatoes, earlier in this chapter)

Blend turkey breast with chopped sage, Canadian bacon and the bread after it has been drained. The mixture should be a little sticky, but you still should be able to form 48 tiny meat balls. Refrigerate.

TO MAKE TORTELLINI DOUGH: Blend flour with eggs and salt. You may mix this by hand or with an electric mixer or food processor. Add 1/4 cup or more water to make a smooth dough. Allow to rest for 10 minutes.

Cut into 4 parts. With a rolling pin or a pasta roller, roll dough thin. Cut into 2-inch round circles with a biscuit or cookie cutter. There should be 48 circles. Cover circles with a damp towel.

TO MAKE TORTELLINI: Place a tiny meatball inside each circle. Fold into the shape of a half moon then fold over to seal filling. Fold ends together, twisting. Slide finished tortellini onto a plate. At this point, tortellini may be wrapped and frozen for up to 1 month.

TO COOK: Heat a large soup pot with 2 quarts water to boil. Add tortellini and cook for 3 to 5 minutes, until dough is just tender.

TO SERVE: Nap plates with 1/3 cup fresh tomato sauce. Arrange 8 tortellini over sauce and dust with parmesan cheese.

Nutritional Information per Serving
Calories 281; Calories from Fat 15%; Total Fat 5 g; Saturated Fat 1 g;
Cholesterol 108 mg; Sodium 392 mg

VEGETABLE LASAGNA

Cook noodles and all vegetables in advance, then make white sauce, grate cheese and assemble.

Serves: 6

1 tablespoon butter
2 cloves garlic, minced
3 cups non-fat milk
4 tablespoons cornstarch
1/2 cup basil leaves
non-stick cooking spray
1/2 pound lasagna noodles, cooked according
   to package directions
1 bunch asparagus, tips only, steamed
1 pound zucchini, sliced and steamed
1 10-ounce package tiny peas, steamed
1 red pepper, sliced and steamed
1/4 cup parmesan cheese, grated
1/2 cup low-fat mozzarella cheese, shredded

In a small saucepan, heat butter, saute garlic. Whisk milk and cornstarch, then add to butter, whisking to make a medium white sauce. Add basil.

TO ASSEMBLE LASGAGNA: Spray a 9 x 13 x 2-inch casserole with non-stick cooking spray. Preheat oven to 400° F. Place 3 cooked noodles on dish and top with 1/3 of the vegetables, 1/3 of the sauce, a dusting of parmesan cheese and 1/3 of mozzarella cheese. Repeat for 2 remaining layers ending with a noodle layer. Top noodle layer with remaining parmesan cheese. Cover with aluminum foil and bake for 20 minutes. Uncover and bake until lasagna is browned, about 10 minutes.

Nutritional Information per Serving
Calories 319; Calories from Fat 19%; Total Fat 7 g; Saturated Fat 4 g;
Cholesterol 9 mg; Sodium 270 mg

VEGETARIAN &

CHAPTER · TWELVE

The wide range of dishes in this chapter use a variety of grains, beans, starchy vegetables and lean vegetables. Vegetarians may want to adapt recipes that call for meat stock by using wine, vegetable stock (see recipe in the Soups & Stews Chapter) or water. Cheese is optional in these recipes, so vegans may simply eliminate this ingredient.

SIDE DISHES

CARIBBEAN-STYLE BLACK BEANS AND RICE

Black beans and rice provide an excellent main course or side dish.

Serves: 6

12 ounces black beans
5 cups vegetable or chicken stock (homemade or prepared)
I tablespoon olive oil
I large onion, chopped
2 green peppers, seeded and chopped into 1/2-inch chunks
2 cloves garlic, minced
1/4 teaspoon ground oregano
I bay leaf
I 1/2 teaspoons ground cumin
1/4 cup lime juice
3 cups cooked rice
6 lime wedges for garnish

In a large bowl, cover beans with water and soak overnight. Drain beans and place in a large soup pot. Cover with stock. Heat to a boil.

Meanwhile, in a large, non-stick frying pan, heat olive oil and saute the onion, green pepper and garlic. Carefully, add these vegetables to hot beans with oregano, bay leaf and cumin. Cover, lower heat to a simmer and cook about I hour, until beans are tender and soup is thick.

Just before serving, add lime juice and salt to taste. Place 1/2 cup rice in large soup bowl. Add bean soup, and garnish with a lime wedge and freshly grated pepper.

Nutritional Information per Serving
Calories 226; Calories from Fat 14%; Total Fat 4 g; Saturated Fat less than I g;
Cholesterol o mg; Sodium 16 mg

EGGPLANT PARMIGIANA

This Eggplant Parmigiana has a delicious and crisp crust with soft and flavorful eggplant inside.

Serves: 6

1 large eggplant (2 pounds)
2 teaspoons salt
1 cup all-purpose flour
1 cup seasoned bread crumbs
1/4 cup parmesan cheese, grated
2 cloves garlic, minced
1 egg
4 egg whites
2 tablespoons oil
non-stick cooking spray
1/2 cup mozzarella cheese, shredded
6 cups cooked spaghetti
4 cups spaghetti sauce (homemade or prepared), heated through

Peel eggplant and slice into 1/2-inch slices. Sprinkle both sides with salt, place in colander and weigh down with plates. This will draw out the moisture, which is important to remove any bitterness and to help the coating adhere.

Put flour into a shallow bowl. Blend bread crumbs, parmesan cheese and garlic and put this mixture into another shallow bowl. Beat egg with egg whites in a third shallow bowl.

Heat oil in a large, non-stick frying pan. Meanwhile, rinse salt from eggplant and pat dry with a paper towel. Coat all slices with flour, eggs and bread crumb mixture. Then saute, a few at a time, in the non-stick pan until both sides are browned.

Coat a baking sheet with non-stick cooking spray. Preheat oven to 375° F. Place eggplant slices on baking sheet, sprinkle with cheese and bake about 15 minutes, until cheese is melted and eggplant is tender.

TO SERVE: Divide spaghetti among warmed plates. Top with sauce, then eggplant slices. Serve immediately.

Nutritional Information per Serving
Calories 442; Calories from Fat 18%; Total Fat 9 g; Saturated Fat 2 g;
Cholesterol 39 mg; Sodium 294 mg

FALAFEL

Falafel combines potatoes and garbanzo beans, two excellent sources of fiber. Cooked falafel may be stored in the refrigerator for 3 days or in the freezer for 2 weeks. Add Hummus (see recipe in Appetizers Chapter) to this pita for a great taste!

Serves: 8

1 teaspoon olive oil
2 cloves garlic, minced
1 medium onion, chopped
3 cups canned garbanzo (or cici) beans,
    drained (24 ounces)
1 large potato, cooked and mashed
    with non-fat milk
1/2 cup cilantro (or parsley), chopped
1/4 cup non-fat yogurt
1/4 teaspoon cayenne pepper
1 teaspoon paprika
juice of 1 lemon
2 tablespoons olive oil
4 whole pitas, halved
lettuce and tomato

In a medium-sized, non-stick frying pan, heat the olive oil. Brown the garlic and onion in oil. Mash the garbanzo beans with a fork or puree in food processor with some of their liquid. Add to browned vegetables. Add the potato, parsley, yogurt, cayenne pepper, paprika and lemon and blend thoroughly. Chill for at least 1 hour.

Form into 24 balls, using about 2 to 2 1/2 tablespoons mix for each ball. Place on baking sheet and bake for 15 minutes.

Heat 2 tablespoons oil in a large, non-stick skillet. Saute the falafel, a few at a time, until well-browned on all sides.

Serve hot in halved pita pockets with shredded lettuce and tomato.

Nutritional Information per Serving
Calories 182; Calories from Fat 20%; Total Fat 4 g; Saturated Fat less than 1 g;
Cholesterol less than 1 mg; Sodium 455 mg

HERBED LEMON COUSCOUS

Couscous is a finely-milled durum wheat which has been steamed and dried. This recipe hints at Middle Eastern flavors and can be enhanced by topping with several shrimp.

Serves: 6

1 teaspoon olive oil
4 cloves garlic, minced
6 scallions, sliced with some green
3 1/2 to 4 cups vegetable or chicken stock
   (homemade or prepared)
2 cups instant couscous, uncooked
1/4 cup chopped mint
juice of 1 lemon

In a medium-sized, non-stick saucepan, heat oil. Saute garlic and scallions until soft. Add 3 cups stock and heat to boiling. Stir in uncooked couscous. Remove from heat and let stand, covered, for 5 minutes. Sprinkle mint and lemon juice over couscous. Fluff with a fork, adding more hot stock if necessary. Serve immediately.

Nutritional Information per Serving
Calories 157; Calories from Fat 11%; Total Fat 2 g; Saturated Fat less than 1 g; Cholesterol 0 mg; Sodium 10 mg

PIEROGIS WITH POTATO-CHEESE FILLING

Once you get the knack of filling these delightful little packages, try other fillings such as sauerkraut, steamed broccoli with a little cheddar or your own leftovers.

Serves: 6 (24 pierogis)

Dough:
4 cups flour
1 teaspoon salt
2 eggs
3/4 to 1 cup (more or less) water

Mashed Potato/Cheese Filling:
2 cups firm, hot, mashed potatoes

2 tablespoons buttermilk
1/4 cup processed cheese
1 tablespoon chives, chopped
2 tablespoons olive oil
1 cup onions, chopped
2 cups low-fat yogurt cheese
1/2 teaspoon paprika

TO MAKE DOUGH: Mix flour and salt, making a "well" in center. Blend eggs with
3/4 cup water and add to flour. Work lightly with hands to form a firm, non-sticky
dough. If necessary, use more water. With a rolling pin, roll the dough to a 1/2-inch
thickness on a floured board. Cut into 3-inch circles. Store in refrigerator with
waxed paper between circles.

Blend mashed potatoes, buttermilk, cheese and chives. Salt and pepper to taste.
Place 1 tablespoon mixture into the bottom half of each circle. Fold over to form a
semi-circle, then crimp edges with a fork to seal. In a large pan, heat 4 cups water
to boiling. Add pierogis and boil until dough is tender, about 10 minutes. Drain
and cool.

Heat oil in a large, non-stick frying pan. Add pierogis and onions, a few at a time,
and lightly brown.

TO SERVE: Place 4 periogis on a warmed plate topped with 1/2-cup yogurt mixture
and a dusting of paprika.

QUICK & EASY: Use won ton wrappers instead of making dough.

Nutritional Information per Serving
Calories 503; Calories from Fat 19%; Total Fat 11 g; Saturated Fat 3 g;
Cholesterol 82 mg; Sodium 548 mg

RATATOUILLE

A traditional vegetarian dish with a little added spice. (see color photo, page 24)

Serves: 6

1 large eggplant, about 2 pounds
1 teaspoon salt
2 tablespoons olive oil
2 large onions, chopped
4 cloves garlic, chopped
1 red pepper, seeded and diced
1 green pepper, seeded and diced
1 small zucchini, sliced
1 yellow squash, sliced
5 large tomatoes, peeled and wedged
2 tablespoons capers with liquid
1 large bunch Italian parsley, chopped
freshly ground black pepper

Peel eggplant and slice into 1/2-inch slices. Sprinkle both sides with salt, place in colander and weigh down with plates. This will draw out the moisture, which is important to remove any bitterness and to help the flavors penetrate the eggplant.

Rinse salt from eggplant and pat dry with a paper towel.

Heat oil in a heavy, non-stick soup pot. Add onion and garlic and saute until soft. Add peppers and cook until they are tender, about 15 minutes. Cube eggplant and add with zucchini, squash and tomatoes.

Simmer for 20 minutes to thicken and blend flavors. Add capers and parsley and cook for an additional 5 minutes. Salt to taste.

Serve in bowls with a sprinkle of black pepper and some crusty French bread.

Nutritional Information per Serving
Calories 65; Calories from Fat 15%; Total Fat 1 g; Saturated Fat less than 1 g;
Cholesterol 4 mg; Sodium 68 mg

RED BEANS AND RICE

This recipe relies on the famous Cajun trio of onion, green pepper and garlic for a wonderful flavor. (see color photo, page 26)

Serves: 4

1/2 pound dry red beans (kidney beans)
4 cups vegetable or chicken stock (homemade or prepared)
1 large yellow onion, chopped
1 large green pepper, chopped
3 ribs celery, chopped
2 cloves garlic, minced
2 bay leaves
1 tablespoon Cajun seasoning
2 cups cooked rice
freshly ground pepper

Cover beans with cold water and soak overnight.

Drain the beans. In a large, non-stick soup pot, heat vegetable stock. Add beans, onion, pepper, celery, garlic, bay leaves and Cajun seasoning. Bring to a boil, reduce heat, cover and simmer for 1 hour.

Continue cooking beans until tender. Watch the pot carefully to prevent the beans from scorching. Add water to pot, as needed to make a thick bean sauce. When beans are tender, remove bay leaves. Salt to taste.

TO SERVE: Divide rice among 4 large bowls. Pour beans over each serving and garnish with a sprinkle of freshly ground black pepper.

Nutritional Information per Serving
Calories 224; Calories from Fat 6%; Total Fat 1 g; Saturated Fat less than 1 g;
Cholesterol 0 mg; Sodium 44 mg

SPINACH LASAGNA

This flavorful recipe makes a lovely presentation.

Serves: 6

non-stick cooking spray
1 tablespoon olive oil
1 large onion, chopped
2 cloves garlic, minced
1 pound spinach, washed 3 times to
　remove sand
1 teaspoon oregano leaves
1 tablespoon fresh basil,
　chopped (or 1 teaspoon
　dried basil)
3 cups spaghetti sauce
　(homemade or prepared)
8 ounces whole-wheat lasagna
　noodles, cooked according to
　package directions
1/2 cup part-skim mozzarella cheese, shredded
1/4 cup parmesan cheese, grated
1 cup low-fat cottage cheese

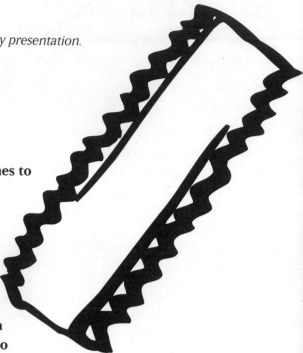

Preheat the oven to 375° F. Spray a 8 x 8-inch baking dish with non-stick cooking spray.

In a large, non-stick saucepan, heat oil. Add onion and garlic and saute until vegetables are translucent. Add spinach 1/3 at a time. Cover. As spinach cooks down, add more spinach. With last batch of spinach, add oregano, basil and spaghetti sauce. Blend thoroughly and remove from heat.

In the bottom of the baking dish, place 1 cup sauce. Place 1/3 noodles on top. Cover with 1 cup sauce and 1/3 of cheeses. Repeat 2 times, ending with cheese attractively sprinkled on top of sauce.

Bake for 40 minutes or until cheeses are well-browned.

Nutritional Information per Serving
Calories 287; Calories from Fat 18%; Total Fat 6 g; Saturated Fat 3 g;
Cholesterol 5 mg; Sodium 438 mg

SUPER BURRITO

An expansive ingredient list makes this burrito truly "super."

Serves: 12

5 1/2 cups vegetable stock
2 cups pinto beans, soaked, and cooked in vegetable stock for 2 hours
2 cups brown rice
2 Anaheim (or other mild) chilis
1 tablespoon olive oil
1 cup onion, sliced
1 cup green pepper, sliced
2 cloves garlic, crushed
2 teaspoons arrano (or other hot chili)
2 tablespoons chili powder
2 teaspoons cumin
12 whole-wheat tortillas
2 cups non-fat yogurt cheese *(see recipe in Appetizers Chapter)*
2 cups Roma tomato, chopped
1/2 cup cilantro, chopped
1/2 cup Anaheim chili, chopped
shredded lettuce and tomato
1/2 cup Monterey jack cheese, shredded

Add rice and Anaheim chili to pinto bean/chicken stock mixture. Simmer for 40 minutes.

In frying pan, heat oil. Add onion, sweet pepper, garlic and arrano chili and saute until transparent. Add chili powder and cumin.

Preheat oven to 350° F. Stir 2 cups rice mixture into vegetable mixture. Divide mixture evenly between tortillas. Fold sides and roll so that burrito is enclosed. Place on a baking sheet and bake for 10 minutes or until tortilla is crispy.

Meanwhile, make cold salsa by combining yogurt with tomato, cilantro and Anaheim chili.

TO SERVE: Place 1 burrito on each plate. Garnish with shredded lettuce, tomato, cheese and salsa.

Nutritional Information per Serving
Calories 294; Calories from Fat 18%; Total Fat 6 g; Saturated Fat 2 g;
Cholesterol 9 mg; Sodium 68 mg

VEGETABLE CURRY

Here's a hot, spicy and nutritious curry.

Serves: 4

8 ounces dry navy beans
2 tablespoons oil
3 medium-sized onions, chopped
5 tablespoons jalapeno peppers, chopped
    (optional)
2 green peppers, seeded and chopped into
    1/4-inch pieces
1 red pepper, seeded and chopped into 1/4-inch pieces
1/4 teaspoon cayenne pepper
1/2 teaspoon white pepper
1 to 3 tablespoons curry powder
3 large, very ripe tomatoes, chopped (or 3 cups canned
    tomatoes with liquid)
1/2 cup frozen corn, thawed and drained
1/2 cup frozen peas, thawed and drained
1 stalk broccoli, stemmed and steamed
2 cups cooked rice
chopped apple, green onions and raisin to top curry

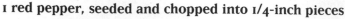

In a medium-sized saucepan, cover the beans with water. Bring to a boil, cover, reduce heat and simmer until beans are tender but not mushy, about 1 1/2 hours.

In a large, non-stick Dutch oven, heat the oil. Saute the onions, peppers, cayenne pepper, white pepper and curry powder for 5 minutes. Add tomatoes to mixture in the Dutch oven. Simmer for 10 minutes. Add the hot beans, corn and peas and heat for 5 minutes until vegetables are hot. Add broccoli and salt and pepper to taste.

TO SERVE: Divide rice among large bowls. Pour curry over rice. Garnish with apple, green onions and raisins.

Nutritional Information per Serving
Calories 408; Calories from Fat 15%; Total Fat 7 g; Saturated Fat less than 1 g;
Cholesterol 0 mg; Sodium 68 mg

VEGETABLE ENCHILADAS

An authentic Tex-Mex recipe. For best results, use hot chili beans or Mexican-style kidney beans.

Serves: 6

non-stick cooking spray
2 teaspoons oil
1 medium-sized onion, minced
1 medium-sized green pepper, chopped into 1/2-inch pieces
1/4 cup fresh cilantro, chopped
2 cups frozen corn, thawed
2 cups zucchini, scrubbed and grated with skin on
1 can (15 ounces) hot chili beans
  (or Mexican-style kidney beans) with liquid
1 teaspoon cumin
1 teaspoon chili powder
12 corn tortillas
1 cup tomato salsa *(see recipe in Appetizers Chapter)*
3 ounces low-fat sharp cheddar cheese, shredded
3 ounces low-fat Monterey jack cheese, shredded

Preheat oven to 350° F. Spray a 9 x 13-inch baking dish with non-stick cooking spray.

In a large skillet, heat the vegetable oil. Saute the onion and green pepper until vegetables are just tender. Add the cilantro, corn and zucchini and heat until zucchini is tender, about 5 minutes. Pour the beans into a small bowl. With the back of a fork, mash the beans in their liquid. Add to vegetables with cumin and chili powder. Stir thoroughly.

Soften the tortillas, if necessary, by wrapping in foil and placing in the preheated oven.

Place 1/3 cup filling in each tortilla. Roll tortillas up and place in baking dish. Cover with salsa and cheeses. Bake until sauce bubbles and cheese melts, about 20 minutes. Salt and pepper to taste.

Nutritional Information per Serving
Calories 326; Calories from Fat 20%; Total Fat 7 g; Saturated Fat 1 g;
Cholesterol 11 mg; Sodium 400 mg

VEGETABLE KABOBS WITH RED PEPPER COULIS

The red pepper coulis gives these kabobs a look all their own.

Serves: 6

Red Pepper Coulis:
1 pound (4 small) red bell peppers, cored, seeded, diced
2 medium tomatoes, peeled and diced
1 large onion, diced
3 cups vegetable or chicken stock
1/2 cup basil, chopped
pinch fresh thyme

The Kabobs:
12 12-inch bamboo skewers
24 small, new potatoes (about 2 pounds),
    well-scrubbed and parboiled for 5 minutes
1 large green pepper, cut into 24 pieces
2 large zucchini, cut into 24 chunks
4 large carrots, peeled and cut into 24 pieces
24 small onions (or 12 medium onions cut in half), about 2 pounds
1 cup tomato juice
1/4 cup fresh basil, chopped
1 teaspoon olive oil
1 teaspoon Dijon mustard
freshly grated pepper

In a saucepan, cook the red pepper, tomato, onion and vegetable stock until vegetables are tender. Stir in basil and thyme. Puree in a blender, then return to saucepan and reduce to about 3 cups.

Thread skewers with vegetables while charcoal or other grill heats. Prepare marinade by blending tomato juice with basil, green onions, olive oil, mustard and pepper. Baste vegetable kabobs with marinade. Place kabobs on grill rack, about 2 inches from heat, and grill, covered, for 6 minutes. Baste with marinade. Turn kabobs
and cook another 6 minutes or until tender, basting frequently.

TO SERVE: Pool 1/2 cup red pepper coulis on each of 6 heated plates; place 2 kabobs on each plate. Spoon a little remaining marinade over each.

Nutritional Information per Serving
Calories 214; Calories from Fat 6%; Total Fat 2 g; Saturated Fat less than 1 g;
Cholesterol 0 mg; Sodium 183 mg

VEGETABLE TACOS WITH FRESH CUCUMBER SALSA

This takes a little work but is well worth the effort. The vegetable sauce reheats well and will last for 1 week in the refrigerator.

Serves: 6

5 pounds pork bones or 6 cups vegetable stock
1 cup canned pinto beans with liquid
1 cup wild rice, uncooked
2 cloves garlic, minced
1 onion, chopped
1 stalk broccoli, cut into flowerettes with stem peeled and chopped
1 1/2 cups yogurt cheese *(see recipe in Appetizers Chapter)*
2 tablespoons dry white wine
2 tablespoons cilantro, chopped
12 taco shells
2 cups Fresh Cucumber Salsa *(see recipe in Appetizers Chapter)*

In a large stockpot, cook bones for 1 hour in 2 quarts water. Defat. Or use 6 cups vegetable stock.

Add beans, wild rice, garlic and onion and heat to boiling. During this time, reduce the stock so that the mixture becomes the consistency of rich chili.
Add broccoli and cook until just tender crisp.

Meanwhile, blend yogurt with wine and cilantro.

TO SERVE: Place 1/2 cup bean/rice mixture in the center of a taco.
Serve with yogurt dressing and Fresh Cucumber Salsa.

Nutritional Information per Serving
Calories 228; Calories from Fat 19%; Total Fat 5 g; Saturated Fat less than 1 g;
Cholesterol less than 1 mg; Sodium 191 mg

CHAPTER · THIRTEEN

"Life's short...eat dessert first." These recipes are perfect for an afternoon treat as well as dessert. Most of the recipes are easy-to-prepare and all are low in fat.

DESSERTS

ALL-AMERICAN PEACH PIE

Here's a slant on an all-American favorite. Great crust!

Serves: 6

Pastry for 8-inch Double Crust:
4 sheets frozen Filo dough, defrosted and wrapped in damp towels
non-stick cooking spray

Peach Filling:
5 cups fresh peaches, pitted and sliced with skins (or a 20-ounce
   package frozen peaches*, not in syrup)
2 teaspoons lemon juice
3/4 cup granulated sugar
1/3 cup all-purpose flour
1/2 teaspoon cinnamon
2 tablespoons margarine

Remove a sheet of Filo dough from damp towel   Double and place over 8 inch-pie plate. Spray a little non-stick cooking spray between layers. Repeat with second sheet of Filo. Trim to fit.

Preheat oven to 375° F. Bake bottom crust for 10 minutes until shell is golden brown.

In a large bowl, combine the peaches with the lemon juice. Add sugar, flour and cinnamon. Toss lightly to mix. Turn into prebaked bottom crust. Dot the peach mixture with margarine.

Remove remaining sheets of Filo dough, double and place over the filling. Spray a little non-stick cooking spray between layers. Trim to fit and flute edges, sealing Filo layers.

Place the pie on a large pan to catch any drips during baking. Bake the pie for 40 minutes or until the juice begins to bubble through slits in the crust. Serve warm.

*If using frozen peaches, increase flour by 1/4 cup.

Nutritional Information per Serving
Calories 176; Calories from Fat 7%; Total Fat 2 g; Saturated Fat less than 1 g;
Cholesterol 0 mg; Sodium 33 mg

ANGEL CAKE

Here's a delicate, whole-grain cake with almost no fat and few calories. For a special treat, serve it with a tangy fruit sauce.

Serves: 12

non-stick cooking spray
1/2 cup whole-wheat pastry flour (if pastry flour is unavailable,
use whole wheat graham flour)
1/2 cup cake flour, sifted
3/4 cup confectioners sugar, sifted
12 large egg whites, room temperature
1 1/2 teaspoons cream of tartar
1/4 teaspoon salt
1 cup granulated sugar
1 1/2 teaspoons vanilla
1/2 teaspoon almond extract

Preheat oven to 375° F. Coat a 10-inch tube pan with non-stick cooking spray.

Blend pastry flour (or graham flour) with sifted cake flour and sifted confectioners sugar. Set aside.

In a large mixing bowl, whip egg whites with the cream of tartar and salt until the mixture is foamy. Sift confectioners sugar, 2 tablespoons at a time, over egg whites, continuing to whip on high speed until stiff peaks form. Make sure all sugar has been incorporated into the egg white. (You can tell this by pinching a bit of the whipped egg white between your fingers; if sugar has been incorporated, you will feel no grains.) Fold in the vanilla and almond extract.

Spoon whole-wheat mixture, 1/4 at a time, over whipped egg whites. Fold in gently until just blended.

Pour batter into the tube pan. Cut gently through the batter with a knife to remove any large bubbles. Bake for 45 minutes or until the crust is golden brown and cracks are very dry. Remove the cake from the oven and invert to cool for 1 hour. Loosen sides and bottom of cake from cake pan. Carefully remove cooled cake from pan.

Nutritional Information per Serving
Calories 136; Calories from Fat 1%; Total Fat less than 1 g; Saturated Fat less than 1 g; Cholesterol 0 mg; Sodium 100 mg

APPLE DUMPLINGS

These warm dumplings are a perfect end to any meal.

Serves: 6

3/4 cups granulated sugar
1/4 teaspoon cinnamon
1/4 teaspoon nutmeg
non-stick cooking spray
1 1/2 cups all-purpose flour
1 teaspoons baking powder
1/4 teaspoon salt
1 1/2 tablespoons oil
2 tablespoons non-fat milk
6 small-sized baking apples, cored
2 tablespoons granulated sugar
1/4 teaspoon cinnamon

TO MAKE THE SYRUP: Combine 3/4 cup sugar with 1/4 teaspoon cinnamon and 1/4 teaspoon nutmeg in a small saucepan. Add 3/4 cup water, bring to boil and cook for 5 minutes. Set syrup aside.

Preheat the oven to 375° F. Spray a 9 x 9 x 2-inch baking dish with non-stick cooking spray.

Combine flour with baking powder and salt. With a pastry blender, cut in oil until the mixture resembles coarse crumbs. Add enough milk to moisten the mixture so that it will form into a ball. Allow the pastry ball to rest for 5 minutes. Divide into 6 parts. On a well-floured cutting board, roll each part with a rolling pin until it is approximately a 4 x 4-inch square.

Place an apple in the center of each square and sprinkle with 2 tablespoons sugar, blended with 1/4 teaspoon cinnamon. Wrap the apple completely with the dough, moistening the edges of the dough and folding corners together so that the apple is completely concealed in dough.

Place in the baking dish. Pour the syrup over the apple dumplings so that it completely wets them. Bake for 45 minutes. The pastry will be crusty and the apples tender. Serve hot or at room temperature.

Nutritional Information per Serving
Calories 307; Calories from Fat 12%; Total Fat 4 g; Saturated Fat less than 1 g;
Cholesterol less than 1 mg; Sodium 360 mg

APPLESAUCE CAKE

This is a very moist cake that is even better the second day.

Serves: 12

non-stick cooking spray
3/4 cup raisins
2 1/4 cups all-purpose flour
1 teaspoon salt
1 1/2 teaspoons baking soda
1 teaspoon cinnamon
1/2 teaspoon ground cloves
1 tablespoon walnuts, toasted and
   chopped
1 cup brown sugar, packed
1/2 cup light margarine
2 tablespoons granulated sugar
1/2 teaspoon grated lemon peel
1 egg, beaten
1 1/2 cups natural applesauce

Preheat oven to 325° F. Spray a 10 x 10 x 2-inch baking pan with non-stick cooking spray.

Plump raisins by steaming them over boiling water for 5 minutes.

Meanwhile, sift flour, then measure. Sift with salt, soda, cinnamon and cloves. Blend 1/4 cup flour mixture with raisins and walnuts.

Cream margarine. Add sugar; cream until well-blended. Add lemon and egg.

Add flour to creamed mixture alternately with applesauce. When well-blended, add raisin-nut mixture.

Pour into prepared pan, pushing the batter a little higher around the edges than in the middle. Bake for 40 minutes, until cake tests done. Cool in the pan for 10 minutes before removing from pan.

Nutritional Information per Serving
Calories 230; Calories from Fat 19%; Total Fat 5 g; Saturated Fat less than 1 g;
Cholesterol 18 mg; Sodium 345 mg

BLUEBERRY COBBLER

*Blueberries, not alternate fruits,
work best for this cobbler.*

Serves: 6

non-stick cooking spray
1 quart fresh blueberries, washed
   and drained
1/3 cup granulated sugar
juice of 1 lemon
1 cup all-purpose flour
1 teaspoon baking powder
1/4 teaspoon salt
1/4 teaspoon allspice
1 teaspoon cinnamon
1/4 cup oil
1/3 cup granulated sugar
1/2 teaspoon vanilla
1/2 cup low-fat milk
1 tablespoon sugar

Preheat oven to 400° F. Spray a 2-quart baking dish with non-stick cooking spray.
Spread the blueberries in the baking dish. Sprinkle them evenly with
1/3 cup of sugar and the lemon juice.

Blend flour with the baking powder, salt, allspice and cinnamon. Blend the oil
with the sugar and vanilla. Add the flour mixture to oil mixture alternately with
the milk. Beat until smooth. Spread over the berries. Sprinkle top with
1 tablespoon sugar.

Bake for 40 minutes until topping is well-browned
and center is firm. Serve warm.

Nutritional Information per Serving
Calories 258; Calories from Fat 15%; Total Fat 5 g;
Saturated Fat less than 1 g; Cholesterol less than 1 mg;
Sodium 249 mg

CARROT CAKE

Years ago, carrot cakes were laden with fat and sugar. This carrot cake is light, moist, delicious and low-fat.

Serves: 15

non-stick cooking spray
2 cups all-purpose flour
1 cup granulated sugar
1 teaspoon baking powder
1 teaspoon baking soda
1 teaspoon salt
1 teaspoon ground cinnamon
1/2 teaspoon cloves
1 cup apple juice
3 cups carrot, finely shredded
1/3 cup light margarine
4 large egg whites
1 8-ounce package fat-free cream cheese, softened
2 tablespoons corn syrup
1 teaspoon vanilla
1 cup sifted confectioners sugar

Preheat oven to 325° F. Spray a 13 x 9 x 2-inch baking pan with non-stick cooking spray.

In a mixing bowl, combine flour with sugar, baking powder, baking soda, salt, cinnamon and cloves. Add the apple juice, carrots, oil and egg whites. Beat at low speed with an electric mixer until the ingredients are combined. Then, beat on medium speed for 2 minutes.

Pour into the prepared pan, pushing the batter a little higher around the edges than in the middle. Bake for 60 minutes or until the center of the cake is firm to touch. Cool.

Combine the cream cheese with the corn syrup and vanilla. Gradually add the confectioners sugar and beat until smooth. Spread the cooled cake with the cream cheese frosting.

Nutritional Information per Serving
Calories 189; Calories from Fat 11%; Total Fat 2 g; Saturated Fat less than 1 g;
Cholesterol less than 1 mg; Sodium 295 mg

CHOCOLATE BANANA BROWNIES

This brownie is packed with nutrition and flavor.

Serves: 16

non-stick cooking spray
4 tablespoons cocoa powder
1 very ripe banana
1 cup granulated sugar
2 large egg whites
1 teaspoon vanilla extract
1/4 teaspoon salt
1 1/2 cups all-purpose flour

Preheat oven to 350° F. Spray an 8-inch round or square cake pan with non-stick cooking spray.

Place the cocoa, 1/4 cup water and the bananas into a large blender cup or into the bowl of a food processor fitted with a steel blade. Blend until smooth. Add the sugar, the egg whites, vanilla extract and salt and blend until the mixture is smooth. Add the flour and 1/2 cup water, a little at a time, and blend until it is smooth.

Pour the chocolate mixture into prepared pan. Bake for 20 to 25 minutes. Wait until the brownies have cooled to cut into squares. Store brownies in the refrigerator.

Nutritional Information per Serving
Calories 107; Calories from Fat 4%; Total Fat less than 1 g;
Saturated Fat less than 1 g; Cholesterol 0 mg; Sodium 63 mg

FRUIT ICES

So easy, fruit ices are a tasty and light way to end a meal.

Serves: 6

1 10-ounce package mixed frozen fruit with syrup
juice of 1/2 lemon
1/2 cup orange juice

Defrost frozen fruit. Blend with fruit juices in a food processor or blender cup. Pour into 6 serving glasses and freeze until solid.

Nutritional Information per Serving
Calories 114; Calories from Fat 1%; Total Fat less than 1 g; Saturated Fat less than 1 g; Cholesterol 0 mg; Sodium 4 mg

FRESH-FRUIT MOUSSE

Make this tangy mousse the day before serving.

Serves: 4

1 envelope unflavored gelatin
1/3 cup granulated sugar
juice of a lemon or lime
2 cups fresh fruit
2 egg whites, room temperature
1 tablespoon sugar

In a small saucepan, dissolve the gelatin in 1/4 cup water. Whisk until smooth. Add sugar and stir until dissolved. Pour into a medium-sized bowl and allow to start to gel.

Meanwhile, puree fresh fruit, lemon or lime and 2 tablespoons water. Whisk fruit mixture into gelatin mixture. Refrigerate for 30 minutes.

Beat egg whites until frothy. Sprinkle sugar over egg whites a little at a time, making sure to incorporate all the sugar. Blend stiffly beaten egg whites with gelatin mixture.

Pour into serving bowl or into individual serving dishes. Refrigerate overnight.

Nutritional Information per Serving
Calories 131; Calories from Fat 2%; Total Fat less than 1 g; Saturated Fat less than 1 g; Cholesterol 0 mg; Sodium 31 mg

STRAWBERRY TART

Here's a tart that will please everyone, with a flaky crust, a sweet cream filling and gorgeous strawberries on top. (see color photo, page 21)

Serves: 6

Pastry for 9-inch Single Crust:
1 to 1 1/4 cups all-purpose flour
1 teaspoon baking powder
1/3 teaspoon salt
1/4 cup oil
1/3 to 1/2 cup buttermilk

Strawberry Cream Filling:
3 egg whites
3/4 cup granulated sugar
3 tablespoons corn starch
2 teaspoons vanilla extract
1 quart firm, ripe strawberries, cleaned and hulled
1/2 cup currant jelly

In a mixing bowl, blend the all-purpose flour and salt. Mix thoroughly. Using a pastry blender, cut in the oil, until mixture has a coarse texture. Sprinkle the milk over the dough and blend until the mixture holds together well. Wet the surface of the counter and place a piece of plastic wrap on the wet counter. Preheat oven to 400° F. Sprinkle plastic wrap with all-purpose flour. Place a ball of pastry on the plastic wrap and sprinkle with more all-purpose flour. Top the sprinkled pastry with a second piece of plastic wrap. Roll with rolling pin until the pastry is slightly larger than 9-inch pie pan. Remove one side of the plastic wrap and fit pastry into pie. Bake for 10 minutes or until crust is well-browned.

In a medium-sized mixing bowl, beat egg whites with sugar until just blended. Whisk corn starch with egg whites a little at a time, to make a smooth paste. Bring milk to just below the boiling point. Remove from heat. Dribble a small amount of milk into the egg white mixture, allowing it to heat. Add heated egg mixture into milk mixture, whisking to keep the sauce clear. Add vanilla and cool.

Melt jelly over crust. Pour filling into piecrust. Top with strawberries arranged in an attractive pattern. Coat strawberries with remaining jelly. Refrigerate until cool. Serve cold or at room temperature.

Nutritional Information for Serving
Calories 316; Calories from Fat 20%; Total Fat less than 7 gg; Saturated Fat less than 1 g; Cholesterol 1 mg; Sodium 196 mg

MERINGUE SHELLS WITH FRESH FRUIT

This elegant dessert is so delicious yet so low in fat.

Serves: 6

1 piece 12 x 16-inch brown paper (a paper bag works fine)
6 egg whites, room temperature
1/2 teaspoon cream of tartar
1/3 cup granulated sugar
3 cups fresh fruit
6 mint sprigs

Preheat oven to 200° F. Place brown paper on a baking sheet.

Whip egg whites with an electric mixer. Blend in cream of tartar.
When egg whites are frothy, sprinkle sugar a teaspoon at a time over egg whites.
Continue to beat egg whites until stiff, incorporating sugar well.

Divide into 6 portions on the paper. Make a well into each.
Bake for 8 hours.

TO SERVE: Carefully remove meringue shells from paper. Place onto small dessert plates. Spoon in fruit and top with a mint sprig.

Nutritional Information per Serving
Calories 81; Calories from Fat 3%;
Total Fat less than 1 g;
Saturated Fat less than 1 g; Cholesterol 0 mg;
Sodium 56 mg

OATMEAL-RAISIN DROP COOKIES

Freshly grinding the cinnamon and nutmeg, using mortar and pestle, makes this old-favorite recipe especially flavorful and unique.

Makes 36 cookies

non-stick cooking spray
1 cup raisins
1 1/2 cups all-purpose flour
1 teaspoon baking soda
1/4 teaspoon salt
1 teaspoon cinnamon
1/2 teaspoon nutmeg
1/2 cup light margarine
1 cup sugar
2 egg whites
2/3 cup buttermilk
1 1/2 cups oatmeal
2 tablespoons walnuts, toasted, finely-chopped

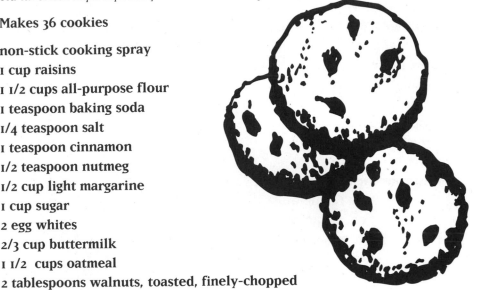

Preheat oven to 375° F. Spray baking sheets with non-stick cooking spray.

Plump raisins by steaming over boiling water for 5 minutes.

Sift flour. Measure, then sift with soda, salt, cinnamon and nutmeg.
Cream margarine with sugar and egg whites until mixture is smooth and fluffy.

Add flour mixture and buttermilk, alternately, to the egg-white mixture.
Blend until very smooth. Add oatmeal, raisins and the nuts. Stir to blend.

Drop by heaping teaspoonfuls onto prepared sheets. Bake for 10 to 12 minutes.
Cookies will be evenly browned.

Nutritional Information per Serving
Calories 90; Calories from Fat 20%; Total Fat 2 g; Saturated Fat less than 1 g;
Cholesterol less than 1 mg; Sodium 120 mg

RICE PUDDING

Smooth and rich tasting, this recipe is also low in fat.

Serves: 6

1 cup raw brown rice, cooked according to package directions
1 cup non-fat evaporated milk
1/2 cup granulated sugar
1 teaspoon cinnamon
1/4 teaspoon allspice
1/4 teaspoon nutmeg
1 cup raisins
4 egg whites
2 tablespoons sugar

Preheat oven to 300° F.

Combine cooked rice with milk, sugar, cinnamon, allspice, nutmeg and raisins.

With an electric mixer or whisk, beat the egg whites until frothy. Add the sugar, a tablespoon at a time, and continue to beat the egg whites until soft peaks form. Gently fold the egg whites into cooled rice mixture, then pour mixture into a 9 x 9-inch square, ungreased baking dish. Bake 20 to 30 minutes until rice is set.

Serve with fresh fruit or fruit sauce.

Nutritional Information per Serving
Calories 276; Calories from Fat 4%; Total Fat 1 g; Saturated Fat less than 1 g;
Cholesterol 2 mg; Sodium 91 mg

SUGAR COOKIES

These quick and easy cookies keep beautifully and are great to have on hand for snacks.

Makes 30 cookies

non-stick cooking spray
2 1/2 cups all-purpose flour
1/2 teaspoon baking soda
1/2 teaspoon salt
3 tablespoons light margarine
3 tablespoons oil
1/4 cup apple juice
1/2 cup granulated sugar
2 egg whites
1 teaspoon vanilla

Preheat oven to 400° F. Spray cookie sheet with non-stick cooking spray.

Combine flour with soda and salt. With an electric mixer, blend the margarine with the oil. Add apple juice, sugar, egg whites and vanilla; beat well. Add the dry ingredients to wet ingredients and blend well.

Drop by teaspoons, 2 inches apart, onto prepared cookie sheet. Bake for 8 to 10 minutes. Cookies will be lightly browned and firm to touch. Remove carefully and cool thoroughly before storing.

Nutritional Information per Cookie
Calories 66; Calories from Fat 17%; Total Fat 1 g; Saturated Fat less than 1 g;
Cholesterol 0 mg; Sodium 81 mg

INDEX